UNCOVER JOHN

I remember the night vividly. Lying awake after an evening with friends, I realised I had just about everything I'd been working for. I should have felt happy and fulfilled. Yet I was plagued with questions: Is this all that life is? Does life have any greater meaning? And any sense of contentment evaporated in to the darkness.

I went on to the next thing and the next, but in the end I kept coming back to that one question: is life meaningless, a blind product of matter plus time plus chance, or is there something more?

I was given a copy of the gospel of John (an account of Jesus' life) by a friend. I knew a little bit about Jesus but had never read any of the ancient texts. I sat down to read with both barrels of my scepticism fully loaded.

I wasn't prepared for Jesus. Wasn't he a moral teacher? So why did religious people try and tear him to pieces? Surely dead men rot in their graves, but Jesus ruined every funeral he went to. I expected boring religion but Jesus promised to give life in all its fullness to all who followed him.

It may be that you too have questions. Perhaps you have never looked into what Jesus said and did. This biography of Jesus was written by John, an eyewitness of the events and one of Jesus' closest friends.

You don't have to believe that the Bible is a sacred text or be a religious person to read this book. Simply approach the text as you would any reliable historical document, with an open mind, willing to follow where the evidence leads. If you have questions about the historical accuracy of John's account you can watch the video below for more information.

At the end of this book you will find six studies, written to help you get a more detailed sense of who Jesus is. Why not go through these studies with a friend. You will also find in the text URL links to videos that will help you engage with the studies. You can find these videos online, along with other resources at uncover.org.uk/john.

Why not take this opportunity to see for yourself who Jesus is and why so many people around the world believe that through Jesus they have uncovered life.

Tim Rudge, UCCF: The Christian Unions

| **Hr** | CAN WE TRUST JOHN'S GOSPEL? |
| URL | uncover. org.uk/john/reliable |

The Gospel of _____ JOHN _____

The Word became flesh

1 In the beginning was the Word, and the Word was with God, and the Word was God. ²He was with God in the beginning. ³Through him all things were made; without him nothing was made that has been made. ⁴In him was life, and that life was the light of all mankind. ⁵The light shines in the darkness, and the darkness has not overcome it.

⁶There was a man sent from God whose name was John. ⁷He came as a witness to testify concerning that light, so that through him all might believe. ⁸He himself was not the light; he came only as a witness to the light.

⁹The true light that gives light to everyone was coming into the world. ¹⁰He was in the world, and though the world was made through him, the world did not recognise him. ¹¹He came to that which was his own, but his own did not receive him. ¹²Yet to all who did receive him, to those who believed in his name, he gave the right to become children of God – ¹³children born not of natural descent, nor of human decision or a husband's will, but born of God.

¹⁴The Word became flesh and made his dwelling among us. We have seen his glory, the glory of the one and only Son, who came from the Father, full of grace and truth.

¹⁵(John testified concerning him. He cried out, saying, 'This is the one I spoke about when I said, "He who comes after me has surpassed me because he was before me." ') ¹⁶Out of his fullness we have all received grace in place of grace already given. ¹⁷For the law was given through Moses; grace and truth came through Jesus Christ. ¹⁸No one has ever seen God, but the one and only Son, who is himself God and is in the closest relationship with the Father, has made him known.

JOHN 1:1

John's first words echo the Bible's account of creation. What does that suggest about the scale of the story he wants to tell?

John the Baptist denies being the Messiah

¹⁹ Now this was John's testimony when the Jewish leaders in Jerusalem sent priests and Levites to ask him who he was. ²⁰ He did not fail to confess, but confessed freely, 'I am not the Messiah.'

²¹ They asked him, 'Then who are you? Are you Elijah?'

He said, 'I am not.'

'Are you the Prophet?'

He answered, 'No.'

²² Finally they said, 'Who are you? Give us an answer to take back to those who sent us. What do you say about yourself?'

²³ John replied in the words of Isaiah the prophet, 'I am the voice of one calling in the wilderness, "Make straight the way for the Lord."'

²⁴ Now the Pharisees who had been sent ²⁵ questioned him, 'Why then do you baptise if you are not the Messiah, nor Elijah, nor the Prophet?'

²⁶ 'I baptise with water,' John replied, 'but among you stands one you do not know. ²⁷ He is the one who comes after me, the straps of whose sandals I am not worthy to untie.'

²⁸ This all happened at Bethany on the other side of the Jordan, where John was baptising.

John testifies about Jesus

²⁹ The next day John saw Jesus coming towards him and said, 'Look, the Lamb of God, who takes away the sin of the world! ³⁰ This is the one I meant when I said, "A man who comes after me has surpassed me because he was before me." ³¹ I myself did not know him, but the reason I came baptising with water was that he might be revealed to Israel.'

³² Then John gave this testimony: 'I saw the Spirit come down from heaven as a dove and remain on him. ³³ And I myself did not know him, but the one who sent me to baptise

with water told me, "The man on whom you see the Spirit come down and remain is the one who will baptise with the Holy Spirit." [34] I have seen and I testify that this is God's Chosen One.'

John's disciples follow Jesus

[35] The next day John was there again with two of his disciples. [36] When he saw Jesus passing by, he said, 'Look, the Lamb of God!'

[37] When the two disciples heard him say this, they followed Jesus. [38] Turning round, Jesus saw them following and asked, 'What do you want?'

They said, 'Rabbi' (which means 'Teacher'), 'where are you staying?'

[39] 'Come,' he replied, 'and you will see.'

So they went and saw where he was staying, and they spent that day with him. It was about four in the afternoon.

[40] Andrew, Simon Peter's brother, was one of the two who heard what John had said and who had followed Jesus. [41] The first thing Andrew did was to find his brother Simon and tell him, 'We have found the Messiah' (that is, the Christ). [42] And he brought him to Jesus.

Jesus looked at him and said, 'You are Simon son of John. You will be called Cephas' (which, when translated, is Peter).

Jesus calls Philip and Nathanael

[43] The next day Jesus decided to leave for Galilee. Finding Philip, he said to him, 'Follow me.'

[44] Philip, like Andrew and Peter, was from the town of Bethsaida. [45] Philip found Nathanael and told him, 'We have found the one Moses wrote about in the Law, and about whom the prophets also wrote – Jesus of Nazareth, the son of Joseph.'

JOHN 1:51

Jesus is claiming to be the
access point to heaven itself.
What would persuade you
that is true?

46'Nazareth! Can anything good come from there?' Nathanael asked.

'Come and see,' said Philip.

47When Jesus saw Nathanael approaching, he said of him, 'Here truly is an Israelite in whom there is no deceit.'

48'How do you know me?' Nathanael asked.

Jesus answered, 'I saw you while you were still under the fig-tree before Philip called you.'

49Then Nathanael declared, 'Rabbi, you are the Son of God; you are the king of Israel.'

50Jesus said, 'You believe because I told you I saw you under the fig-tree. You will see greater things than that.' 51He then added, 'Very truly I tell you, you will see "heaven open, and the angels of God ascending and descending on" the Son of Man.'

Jesus changes water into wine

2 On the third day a wedding took place at Cana in Galilee. Jesus' mother was there, 2and Jesus and his disciples had also been invited to the wedding. 3When the wine was gone, Jesus' mother said to him, 'They have no more wine.'

4'Woman, why do you involve me?' Jesus replied. 'My hour has not yet come.'

5His mother said to the servants, 'Do whatever he tells you.'

6Nearby stood six stone water jars, the kind used by the Jews for ceremonial washing, each holding from eighty to a hundred and twenty litres.

7Jesus said to the servants, 'Fill the jars with water'; so they filled them to the brim.

8Then he told them, 'Now draw some out and take it to the master of the banquet.'

They did so, 9and the master of the banquet tasted the

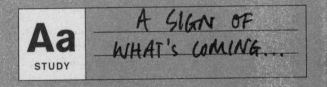

Aa
STUDY

A SIGN OF WHAT'S COMING...

In his book *The Last Word*, author Thomas Nagel writes, 'I want atheism to be true, and I am made uneasy by the fact that some of the most intelligent and well informed people I know are religious believers. It isn't just that I don't believe in God and, naturally, hope that I'm right in my belief. It is that I hope there is no God. I don't want there to be a God, I don't want the universe to be like that.'

Why might someone 'hope there is no God'?

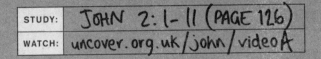

STUDY: JOHN 2: 1-11 (PAGE 126)
WATCH: uncover.org.uk/john/videoA

water that had been turned into wine. He did not realise where it had come from, though the servants who had drawn the water knew. Then he called the bridegroom aside ¹⁰ and said, 'Everyone brings out the choice wine first and then the cheaper wine after the guests have had too much to drink; but you have saved the best till now.'

¹¹ What Jesus did here in Cana of Galilee was the first of the signs through which he revealed his glory; and his disciples believed in him.

¹² After this he went down to Capernaum with his mother and brothers and his disciples. There they stayed for a few days.

Jesus clears the temple courts

¹³ When it was almost time for the Jewish Passover, Jesus went up to Jerusalem. ¹⁴ In the temple courts he found people selling cattle, sheep and doves, and others sitting at tables exchanging money. ¹⁵ So he made a whip out of cords, and drove all from the temple courts, both sheep and cattle; he scattered the coins of the money-changers and overturned their tables. ¹⁶ To those who sold doves he said, 'Get these out of here! Stop turning my Father's house into a market!' ¹⁷ His disciples remembered that it is written: 'Zeal for your house will consume me.'

¹⁸ The Jews then responded to him, 'What sign can you show us to prove your authority to do all this?'

¹⁹ Jesus answered them, 'Destroy this temple, and I will raise it again in three days.'

²⁰ They replied, 'It has taken forty-six years to build this temple, and you are going to raise it in three days?' ²¹ But the temple he had spoken of was his body. ²² After he was raised from the dead, his disciples recalled what he had said. Then they believed the Scripture and the words that Jesus had spoken.

JOHN 2:21

Jesus links his authority to
radically reform the temple
to his resurrection

23 Now while he was in Jerusalem at the Passover Festival, many people saw the signs he was performing and believed in his name. 24 But Jesus would not entrust himself to them, for he knew all people. 25 He did not need any testimony about mankind, for he knew what was in each person.

Jesus teaches Nicodemus

3 Now there was a Pharisee, a man named Nicodemus who was a member of the Jewish ruling council. 2 He came to Jesus at night and said, 'Rabbi, we know that you are a teacher who has come from God. For no one could perform the signs you are doing if God were not with him.'

3 Jesus replied, 'Very truly I tell you, no one can see the kingdom of God unless they are born again.'

4 'How can someone be born when they are old?' Nicodemus asked. 'Surely they cannot enter a second time into their mother's womb to be born!'

5 Jesus answered, 'Very truly I tell you, no one can enter the kingdom of God unless they are born of water and the Spirit. 6 Flesh gives birth to flesh, but the Spirit gives birth to spirit. 7 You should not be surprised at my saying, "You must be born again." 8 The wind blows wherever it pleases. You hear its sound, but you cannot tell where it comes from or where it is going. So it is with everyone born of the Spirit.'

9 'How can this be?' Nicodemus asked.

10 'You are Israel's teacher,' said Jesus, 'and do you not understand these things? 11 Very truly I tell you, we speak of what we know, and we testify to what we have seen, but still you people do not accept our testimony. 12 I have spoken to you of earthly things and you do not believe; how then will you believe if I speak of heavenly things? 13 No one has ever gone into heaven except the one who came from heaven – the Son of Man. 14 Just as Moses lifted up the snake in the

JOHN 3:3

What do you make of Jesus' claim that each of us requires radical transformation?

wilderness, so the Son of Man must be lifted up, ¹⁵that everyone who believes may have eternal life in him.'

¹⁶For God so loved the world that he gave his one and only Son, that whoever believes in him shall not perish but have eternal life. ¹⁷For God did not send his Son into the world to condemn the world, but to save the world through him. ¹⁸Whoever believes in him is not condemned, but whoever does not believe stands condemned already because they have not believed in the name of God's one and only Son. ¹⁹This is the verdict: light has come into the world, but people loved darkness instead of light because their deeds were evil. ²⁰Everyone who does evil hates the light, and will not come into the light for fear that their deeds will be exposed. ²¹But whoever lives by the truth comes into the light, so that it may be seen plainly that what they have done has been done in the sight of God.

John testifies again about Jesus

²²After this, Jesus and his disciples went out into the Judean countryside, where he spent some time with them, and baptised. ²³Now John also was baptising at Aenon near Salim, because there was plenty of water, and people were coming and being baptised. ²⁴(This was before John was put in prison.) ²⁵An argument developed between some of John's disciples and a certain Jew over the matter of ceremonial washing. ²⁶They came to John and said to him, 'Rabbi, that man who was with you on the other side of the Jordan – the one you testified about – look, he is baptising, and everyone is going to him.'

²⁷To this John replied, 'A person can receive only what is given them from heaven. ²⁸You yourselves can testify that I said, "I am not the Messiah but am sent ahead of him." ²⁹The bride belongs to the bridegroom. The friend who attends the bridegroom waits and listens for him, and is full of joy when

he hears the bridegroom's voice. That joy is mine, and it is now complete. ³⁰ He must become greater; I must become less.'

³¹ The one who comes from above is above all; the one who is from the earth belongs to the earth, and speaks as one from the earth. The one who comes from heaven is above all. ³² He testifies to what he has seen and heard, but no one accepts his testimony. ³³ Whoever has accepted it has certified that God is truthful. ³⁴ For the one whom God has sent speaks the words of God, for God gives the Spirit without limit. ³⁵ The Father loves the Son and has placed everything in his hands. ³⁶ Whoever believes in the Son has eternal life, but whoever rejects the Son will not see life, for God's wrath remains on them.

Jesus talks with a Samaritan woman

4 Now Jesus learned that the Pharisees had heard that he was gaining and baptising more disciples than John – ² although in fact it was not Jesus who baptised, but his disciples. ³ So he left Judea and went back once more to Galilee.

⁴ Now he had to go through Samaria. ⁵ So he came to a town in Samaria called Sychar, near the plot of ground Jacob had given to his son Joseph. ⁶ Jacob's well was there, and Jesus, tired as he was from the journey, sat down by the well. It was about noon.

⁷ When a Samaritan woman came to draw water, Jesus said to her, 'Will you give me a drink?' ⁸ (His disciples had gone into the town to buy food.)

⁹ The Samaritan woman said to him, 'You are a Jew and I am a Samaritan woman. How can you ask me for a drink?' (For Jews do not associate with Samaritans.)

¹⁰ Jesus answered her, 'If you knew the gift of God and who it is that asks you for a drink, you would have asked him and he would have given you living water.'

Bb
STUDY

DO YOU COME HERE OFTEN?

'Resign yourself to the lifelong sadness that comes from never being satisfied.' Like many people, successful author Zadie Smith has found satisfaction elusive.

Do you think it is possible to find lasting satisfaction, and, if so, how?

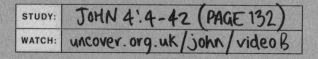

STUDY: JOHN 4:4-42 (PAGE 132)

WATCH: uncover.org.uk/john/video B

¹¹ 'Sir,' the woman said, 'you have nothing to draw with and the well is deep. Where can you get this living water? ¹² Are you greater than our father Jacob, who gave us the well and drank from it himself, as did also his sons and his livestock?'

¹³ Jesus answered, 'Everyone who drinks this water will be thirsty again, ¹⁴ but whoever drinks the water I give them will never thirst. Indeed, the water I give them will become in them a spring of water welling up to eternal life.'

¹⁵ The woman said to him, 'Sir, give me this water so that I won't get thirsty and have to keep coming here to draw water.'

¹⁶ He told her, 'Go, call your husband and come back.'

¹⁷ 'I have no husband,' she replied.

Jesus said to her, 'You are right when you say you have no husband. ¹⁸ The fact is, you have had five husbands, and the man you now have is not your husband. What you have just said is quite true.'

¹⁹ 'Sir,' the woman said, 'I can see that you are a prophet. ²⁰ Our ancestors worshipped on this mountain, but you Jews claim that the place where we must worship is in Jerusalem.'

²¹ 'Woman,' Jesus replied, 'believe me, a time is coming when you will worship the Father neither on this mountain nor in Jerusalem. ²² You Samaritans worship what you do not know; we worship what we do know, for salvation is from the Jews. ²³ Yet a time is coming and has now come when the true worshippers will worship the Father in the Spirit and in truth, for they are the kind of worshippers the Father seeks. ²⁴ God is spirit, and his worshippers must worship in the Spirit and in truth.'

²⁵ The woman said, 'I know that Messiah' (called Christ) 'is coming. When he comes, he will explain everything to us.'

²⁶ Then Jesus declared, 'I, the one speaking to you – I am he.'

The disciples rejoin Jesus

²⁷ Just then his disciples returned and were surprised to find him talking with a woman. But no one asked, 'What do you want?' or 'Why are you talking with her?'

²⁸ Then, leaving her water jar, the woman went back to the town and said to the people, ²⁹ 'Come, see a man who told me everything I've ever done. Could this be the Messiah?' ³⁰ They came out of the town and made their way towards him.

³¹ Meanwhile his disciples urged him, 'Rabbi, eat something.'

³² But he said to them, 'I have food to eat that you know nothing about.'

³³ Then his disciples said to each other, 'Could someone have brought him food?'

³⁴ 'My food,' said Jesus, 'is to do the will of him who sent me and to finish his work. ³⁵ Don't you have a saying, "It's still four months until harvest"? I tell you, open your eyes and look at the fields! They are ripe for harvest. ³⁶ Even now the one who reaps draws a wage and harvests a crop for eternal life, so that the sower and the reaper may be glad together. ³⁷ Thus the saying "One sows and another reaps" is true. ³⁸ I sent you to reap what you have not worked for. Others have done the hard work, and you have reaped the benefits of their labour.'

Many Samaritans believe

³⁹ Many of the Samaritans from that town believed in him because of the woman's testimony, 'He told me everything I've ever done.' ⁴⁰ So when the Samaritans came to him, they urged him to stay with them, and he stayed two days. ⁴¹ And because of his words many more became believers.

⁴² They said to the woman, 'We no longer believe just because of what you said; now we have heard for ourselves, and we know that this man really is the Saviour of the world.'

Jesus heals an official's son

43 After the two days he left for Galilee. 44 (Now Jesus himself had pointed out that a prophet has no honour in his own country.) 45 When he arrived in Galilee, the Galileans welcomed him. They had seen all that he had done in Jerusalem at the Passover Festival, for they also had been there.

46 Once more he visited Cana in Galilee, where he had turned the water into wine. And there was a certain royal official whose son lay ill at Capernaum. 47 When this man heard that Jesus had arrived in Galilee from Judea, he went to him and begged him to come and heal his son, who was close to death.

48 'Unless you people see signs and wonders,' Jesus told him, 'you will never believe.'

49 The royal official said, 'Sir, come down before my child dies.'

50 'Go,' Jesus replied, 'your son will live.'

The man took Jesus at his word and departed. 51 While he was still on the way, his servants met him with the news that his boy was living. 52 When he enquired as to the time when his son got better, they said to him, 'Yesterday, at one in the afternoon, the fever left him.'

53 Then the father realised that this was the exact time at which Jesus had said to him, 'Your son will live.' So he and his whole household believed.

54 This was the second sign Jesus performed after coming from Judea to Galilee.

JOHN 4:48

→ What might be a reason to believe
other than signs + wonders?

The healing at the pool

5 Some time later, Jesus went up to Jerusalem for one of the Jewish festivals. ²Now there is in Jerusalem near the Sheep Gate a pool, which in Aramaic is called Bethesda and which is surrounded by five covered colonnades. ³Here a great number of disabled people used to lie – the blind, the lame, the paralysed. ⁵One who was there had been an invalid for thirty-eight years. ⁶When Jesus saw him lying there and learned that he had been in this condition for a long time, he asked him, 'Do you want to get well?'

⁷'Sir,' the invalid replied, 'I have no one to help me into the pool when the water is stirred. While I am trying to get in, someone else goes down ahead of me.'

⁸Then Jesus said to him, 'Get up! Pick up your mat and walk.' ⁹At once the man was cured; he picked up his mat and walked.

The day on which this took place was a Sabbath, ¹⁰and so the Jewish leaders said to the man who had been healed, 'It is the Sabbath; the law forbids you to carry your mat.'

¹¹But he replied, 'The man who made me well said to me, "Pick up your mat and walk." '

¹²So they asked him, 'Who is this fellow who told you to pick it up and walk?'

¹³The man who was healed had no idea who it was, for Jesus had slipped away into the crowd that was there.

¹⁴Later Jesus found him at the temple and said to him, 'See, you are well again. Stop sinning or something worse may happen to you.' ¹⁵The man went away and told the Jewish leaders that it was Jesus who had made him well.

The authority of the Son

¹⁶So, because Jesus was doing these things on the Sabbath, the Jewish leaders began to persecute him. ¹⁷In his defence Jesus said to them, 'My Father is always at his work to

JOHN 5:16

The Sabbath was intended to be
a day of rest + restoration.
What's ironic about the Jewish
leaders' objection to Jesus' actions?

this very day, and I too am working.' ¹⁸ For this reason they tried all the more to kill him; not only was he breaking the Sabbath, but he was even calling God his own Father, making himself equal with God.

¹⁹ Jesus gave them this answer: 'Very truly I tell you, the Son can do nothing by himself; he can do only what he sees his Father doing, because whatever the Father does the Son also does. ²⁰ For the Father loves the Son and shows him all he does. Yes, and he will show him even greater works than these, so that you will be amazed. ²¹ For just as the Father raises the dead and gives them life, even so the Son gives life to whom he is pleased to give it. ²² Moreover, the Father judges no one, but has entrusted all judgment to the Son, ²³ that all may honour the Son just as they honour the Father. Whoever does not honour the Son does not honour the Father, who sent him.

²⁴ 'Very truly I tell you, whoever hears my word and believes him who sent me has eternal life and will not be judged but has crossed over from death to life. ²⁵ Very truly I tell you, a time is coming and has now come when the dead will hear the voice of the Son of God and those who hear will live. ²⁶ For as the Father has life in himself, so he has granted the Son also to have life in himself. ²⁷ And he has given him authority to judge because he is the Son of Man.

²⁸ 'Do not be amazed at this, for a time is coming when all who are in their graves will hear his voice ²⁹ and come out – those who have done what is good will rise to live, and those who have done what is evil will rise to be condemned. ³⁰ By myself I can do nothing; I judge only as I hear, and my judgment is just, for I seek not to please myself but him who sent me.

JOHN 5:24

Jesus claims that believing his words
can bring real life right now

Testimonies about Jesus

³¹ 'If I testify about myself, my testimony is not true. ³² There is another who testifies in my favour, and I know that his testimony about me is true.

³³ 'You have sent to John and he has testified to the truth. ³⁴ Not that I accept human testimony; but I mention it that you may be saved. ³⁵ John was a lamp that burned and gave light, and you chose for a time to enjoy his light.

³⁶ 'I have testimony weightier than that of John. For the works that the Father has given me to finish – the very works that I am doing – testify that the Father has sent me. ³⁷ And the Father who sent me has himself testified concerning me. You have never heard his voice nor seen his form, ³⁸ nor does his word dwell in you, for you do not believe the one he sent. ³⁹ You study the Scriptures diligently because you think that in them you have eternal life. These are the very Scriptures that testify about me, ⁴⁰ yet you refuse to come to me to have life.

⁴¹ 'I do not accept glory from human beings, ⁴² but I know you. I know that you do not have the love of God in your hearts. ⁴³ I have come in my Father's name, and you do not accept me; but if someone else comes in his own name, you will accept him. ⁴⁴ How can you believe since you accept glory from one another but do not seek the glory that comes from the only God?

⁴⁵ 'But do not think I will accuse you before the Father. Your accuser is Moses, on whom your hopes are set. ⁴⁶ If you believed Moses, you would believe me, for he wrote about me. ⁴⁷ But since you do not believe what he wrote, how are you going to believe what I say?'

Jesus feeds the five thousand

6 Some time after this, Jesus crossed to the far shore of the Sea of Galilee (that is, the Sea of Tiberias), ²and a great crowd of people followed him because they saw the signs he had performed by healing those who were ill. ³Then Jesus went up on a mountainside and sat down with his disciples. ⁴The Jewish Passover Festival was near.

⁵When Jesus looked up and saw a great crowd coming towards him, he said to Philip, 'Where shall we buy bread for these people to eat?' ⁶He asked this only to test him, for he already had in mind what he was going to do.

⁷Philip answered him, 'It would take more than half a year's wages to buy enough bread for each one to have a bite!'

⁸Another of his disciples, Andrew, Simon Peter's brother, spoke up, ⁹'Here is a boy with five small barley loaves and two small fish, but how far will they go among so many?'

¹⁰Jesus said, 'Make the people sit down.' There was plenty of grass in that place, and they sat down (about five thousand men were there). ¹¹Jesus then took the loaves, gave thanks, and distributed to those who were seated as much as they wanted. He did the same with the fish.

¹²When they had all had enough to eat, he said to his disciples, 'Gather the pieces that are left over. Let nothing be wasted.' ¹³So they gathered them and filled twelve baskets with the pieces of the five barley loaves left over by those who had eaten.

¹⁴After the people saw the sign Jesus performed, they began to say, 'Surely this is the Prophet who is to come into the world.' ¹⁵Jesus, knowing that they intended to come and make him king by force, withdrew again to a mountain by himself.

JOHN 6:15

→ Jesus rejects the people's attempt
to make him king. Why do you
think that is?

Jesus walks on the water

16 When evening came, his disciples went down to the lake, 17 where they got into a boat and set off across the lake for Capernaum. By now it was dark, and Jesus had not yet joined them. 18 A strong wind was blowing and the waters grew rough. 19 When they had rowed about three or four miles, they saw Jesus approaching the boat, walking on the water; and they were frightened. 20 But he said to them, 'It is I; don't be afraid.' 21 Then they were willing to take him into the boat, and immediately the boat reached the shore where they were heading.

22 The next day the crowd that had stayed on the opposite shore of the lake realised that only one boat had been there, and that Jesus had not entered it with his disciples, but that they had gone away alone. 23 Then some boats from Tiberias landed near the place where the people had eaten the bread after the Lord had given thanks. 24 Once the crowd realised that neither Jesus nor his disciples were there, they got into the boats and went to Capernaum in search of Jesus.

Jesus the bread of life

25 When they found him on the other side of the lake, they asked him, 'Rabbi, when did you get here?'

26 Jesus answered, 'Very truly I tell you, you are looking for me, not because you saw the signs I performed but because you ate the loaves and had your fill. 27 Do not work for food that spoils, but for food that endures to eternal life, which the Son of Man will give you. For on him God the Father has placed his seal of approval.'

28 Then they asked him, 'What must we do to do the works God requires?'

29 Jesus answered, 'The work of God is this: to believe in the one he has sent.'

30 So they asked him, 'What sign then will you give that

JOHN 6:29

→ Is it really true that all God requires
is to believe in Jesus? what do you think?

we may see it and believe you? What will you do? [31] Our ancestors ate the manna in the wilderness; as it is written: "He gave them bread from heaven to eat."'

[32] Jesus said to them, 'Very truly I tell you, it is not Moses who has given you the bread from heaven, but it is my Father who gives you the true bread from heaven. [33] For the bread of God is the bread that comes down from heaven and gives life to the world.'

[34] 'Sir,' they said, 'always give us this bread.'

[35] Then Jesus declared, 'I am the bread of life. Whoever comes to me will never go hungry, and whoever believes in me will never be thirsty. [36] But as I told you, you have seen me and still you do not believe. [37] All those the Father gives me will come to me, and whoever comes to me I will never drive away. [38] For I have come down from heaven not to do my will but to do the will of him who sent me. [39] And this is the will of him who sent me, that I shall lose none of all those he has given me, but raise them up at the last day. [40] For my Father's will is that everyone who looks to the Son and believes in him shall have eternal life, and I will raise them up at the last day.'

[41] At this the Jews there began to grumble about him because he said, 'I am the bread that came down from heaven.' [42] They said, 'Is this not Jesus, the son of Joseph, whose father and mother we know? How can he now say, "I came down from heaven"?'

[43] 'Stop grumbling among yourselves,' Jesus answered. [44] 'No one can come to me unless the Father who sent me draws them, and I will raise them up at the last day. [45] It is written in the Prophets: "They will all be taught by God." Everyone who has heard the Father and learned from him comes to me. [46] No one has seen the Father except the one who is from God; only he has seen the Father. [47] Very truly I tell you, the one who believes has eternal life.

[48] I am the bread of life. [49] Your ancestors ate the manna in the wilderness, yet they died. [50] But here is the bread that comes down from heaven, which anyone may eat and not die. [51] I am the living bread that came down from heaven. Whoever eats this bread will live for ever. This bread is my flesh, which I will give for the life of the world.'

[52] Then the Jews began to argue sharply among themselves, 'How can this man give us his flesh to eat?'

[53] Jesus said to them, 'Very truly I tell you, unless you eat the flesh of the Son of Man and drink his blood, you have no life in you. [54] Whoever eats my flesh and drinks my blood has eternal life, and I will raise them up at the last day. [55] For my flesh is real food and my blood is real drink. [56] Whoever eats my flesh and drinks my blood remains in me, and I in them. [57] Just as the living Father sent me and I live because of the Father, so the one who feeds on me will live because of me. [58] This is the bread that came down from heaven. Your ancestors ate manna and died, but whoever feeds on this bread will live for ever.' [59] He said this while teaching in the synagogue in Capernaum.

Many disciples desert Jesus

[60] On hearing it, many of his disciples said, 'This is a hard teaching. Who can accept it?'

[61] Aware that his disciples were grumbling about this, Jesus said to them, 'Does this offend you? [62] Then what if you see the Son of Man ascend to where he was before! [63] The Spirit gives life; the flesh counts for nothing. The words I have spoken to you – they are full of the Spirit and life. [64] Yet there are some of you who do not believe.' For Jesus had known from the beginning which of them did not believe and who would betray him. [65] He went on to say, 'This is why I told you that no one can come to me unless the Father has enabled them.'

JOHN 6:54

These are challenging words!
How does v47 help you to
understand what Jesus means?
Why does he use such a
vivid metaphor?

66 From this time many of his disciples turned back and no longer followed him.

67 'You do not want to leave too, do you?' Jesus asked the Twelve.

68 Simon Peter answered him, 'Lord, to whom shall we go? You have the words of eternal life. 69 We have come to believe and to know that you are the Holy One of God.'

70 Then Jesus replied, 'Have I not chosen you, the Twelve? Yet one of you is a devil!' 71 (He meant Judas, the son of Simon Iscariot, who, though one of the Twelve, was later to betray him.)

Jesus goes to the Festival of Tabernacles

7 After this, Jesus went around in Galilee. He did not want to go about in Judea because the Jewish leaders there were looking for a way to kill him. 2 But when the Jewish Festival of Tabernacles was near, 3 Jesus' brothers said to him, 'Leave Galilee and go to Judea, so that your disciples there may see the works you do. 4 No one who wants to become a public figure acts in secret. Since you are doing these things, show yourself to the world.' 5 For even his own brothers did not believe in him.

6 Therefore Jesus told them, 'My time is not yet here; for you any time will do. 7 The world cannot hate you, but it hates me because I testify that its works are evil. 8 You go to the festival. I am not going up to this festival, because my time has not yet fully come.' 9 After he had said this, he stayed in Galilee.

10 However, after his brothers had left for the festival, he went also, not publicly, but in secret. 11 Now at the festival the Jewish leaders were watching for Jesus and asking, 'Where is he?'

12 Among the crowds there was widespread whispering about him. Some said, 'He is a good man.'

JOHN 7:6

Jesus talks about his 'time' as he did
in ch 2 — what do you think this is?
what is central in his thinking?

Others replied, 'No, he deceives the people.' ¹³But no one would say anything publicly about him for fear of the leaders.

Jesus teaches at the festival

¹⁴Not until halfway through the festival did Jesus go up to the temple courts and begin to teach. ¹⁵The Jews there were amazed and asked, 'How did this man get such learning without having been taught?'

¹⁶Jesus answered, 'My teaching is not my own. It comes from the one who sent me. ¹⁷Anyone who chooses to do the will of God will find out whether my teaching comes from God or whether I speak on my own. ¹⁸Whoever speaks on their own does so to gain personal glory, but he who seeks the glory of the one who sent him is a man of truth; there is nothing false about him. ¹⁹Has not Moses given you the law? Yet not one of you keeps the law. Why are you trying to kill me?'

²⁰'You are demon-possessed,' the crowd answered. 'Who is trying to kill you?'

²¹Jesus said to them, 'I did one miracle, and you are all amazed. ²²Yet, because Moses gave you circumcision (though actually it did not come from Moses, but from the patriarchs), you circumcise a boy on the Sabbath. ²³Now if a boy can be circumcised on the Sabbath so that the law of Moses may not be broken, why are you angry with me for healing a man's whole body on the Sabbath? ²⁴Stop judging by mere appearances, but instead judge correctly.'

Division over who Jesus is

²⁵At that point some of the people of Jerusalem began to ask, 'Isn't this the man they are trying to kill? ²⁶Here he is, speaking publicly, and they are not saying a word to him. Have the authorities really concluded that he is the Messiah?

27 But we know where this man is from; when the Messiah comes, no one will know where he is from.'

28 Then Jesus, still teaching in the temple courts, cried out, 'Yes, you know me, and you know where I am from. I am not here on my own authority, but he who sent me is true. You do not know him, 29 but I know him because I am from him and he sent me.'

30 At this they tried to seize him, but no one laid a hand on him, because his hour had not yet come. 31 Still, many in the crowd believed in him. They said, 'When the Messiah comes, will he perform more signs than this man?'

32 The Pharisees heard the crowd whispering such things about him. Then the chief priests and the Pharisees sent temple guards to arrest him.

33 Jesus said, 'I am with you for only a short time, and then I am going to the one who sent me. 34 You will look for me, but you will not find me; and where I am, you cannot come.'

35 The Jews said to one another, 'Where does this man intend to go that we cannot find him? Will he go where our people live scattered among the Greeks, and teach the Greeks? 36 What did he mean when he said, "You will look for me, but you will not find me," and "Where I am, you cannot come"?'

37 On the last and greatest day of the festival, Jesus stood and said in a loud voice, 'Let anyone who is thirsty come to me and drink. 38 Whoever believes in me, as Scripture has said, rivers of living water will flow from within them.' 39 By this he meant the Spirit, whom those who believed in him were later to receive. Up to that time the Spirit had not been given, since Jesus had not yet been glorified.

40 On hearing his words, some of the people said, 'Surely this man is the Prophet.'

41 Others said, 'He is the Messiah.'

JOHN 7:37-39

 Jesus returns to the theme of
thirst + water. His implication is
that only the Spirit of God is
enough to satisfy our desire.

Still others asked, 'How can the Messiah come from Galilee? [42] Does not Scripture say that the Messiah will come from David's descendants and from Bethlehem, the town where David lived?' [43] Thus the people were divided because of Jesus. [44] Some wanted to seize him, but no one laid a hand on him.

Unbelief of the Jewish leaders

[45] Finally the temple guards went back to the chief priests and the Pharisees, who asked them, 'Why didn't you bring him in?'

[46] 'No one ever spoke the way this man does,' the guards replied.

[47] 'You mean he has deceived you also?' the Pharisees retorted. [48] 'Have any of the rulers or of the Pharisees believed in him? [49] No! But this mob that knows nothing of the law – there is a curse on them.'

[50] Nicodemus, who had gone to Jesus earlier and who was one of their own number, asked, [51] 'Does our law condemn a man without first hearing him to find out what he has been doing?'

[52] They replied, 'Are you from Galilee, too? Look into it, and you will find that a prophet does not come out of Galilee.'

[The earliest manuscripts and many other ancient witnesses do not have John 7:53 – 8:11. A few manuscripts include these verses, wholly or in part, after John 7:36, John 21:25, Luke 21:38 or Luke 24:53.]

8 [53] Then they all went home, [1] but Jesus went to the Mount of Olives.

[2] At dawn he appeared again in the temple courts, where all the people gathered round him, and he sat down to teach them. [3] The teachers of the law and the Pharisees brought in a woman caught

JOHN 7:52

The authorities' conflict with Jesus
continues to ratchet up. Who has
your sympathy?

in adultery. They made her stand before the group ⁴*and said to Jesus, 'Teacher, this woman was caught in the act of adultery.* ⁵*In the Law Moses commanded us to stone such women. Now what do you say?'* ⁶*They were using this question as a trap, in order to have a basis for accusing him.*

But Jesus bent down and started to write on the ground with his finger. ⁷When they kept on questioning him, he straightened up and said to them, 'Let any one of you who is without sin be the first to throw a stone at her.' ⁸Again he stooped down and wrote on the ground.

⁹At this, those who heard began to go away one at a time, the older ones first, until only Jesus was left, with the woman still standing there. ¹⁰Jesus straightened up and asked her, 'Woman, where are they? Has no one condemned you?'

¹¹'No one, sir,' she said.

'Then neither do I condemn you,' Jesus declared. 'Go now and leave your life of sin.'

Dispute over Jesus' testimony

¹²When Jesus spoke again to the people, he said, 'I am the light of the world. Whoever follows me will never walk in darkness, but will have the light of life.'

¹³The Pharisees challenged him, 'Here you are, appearing as your own witness; your testimony is not valid.'

¹⁴Jesus answered, 'Even if I testify on my own behalf, my testimony is valid, for I know where I came from and where I am going. But you have no idea where I come from or where I am going. ¹⁵You judge by human standards; I pass judgment on no one. ¹⁶But if I do judge, my decisions are true, because I am not alone. I stand with the Father, who sent me. ¹⁷In your own Law it is written that the testimony of two witnesses is true. ¹⁸I am one who testifies for myself; my other witness is the Father, who sent me.'

¹⁹ Then they asked him, 'Where is your father?'

'You do not know me or my Father,' Jesus replied. 'If you knew me, you would know my Father also.' ²⁰ He spoke these words while teaching in the temple courts near the place where the offerings were put. Yet no one seized him, because his hour had not yet come.

Dispute over who Jesus is

²¹ Once more Jesus said to them, 'I am going away, and you will look for me, and you will die in your sin. Where I go, you cannot come.'

²² This made the Jews ask, 'Will he kill himself? Is that why he says, "Where I go, you cannot come"?'

²³ But he continued, 'You are from below; I am from above. You are of this world; I am not of this world. ²⁴ I told you that you would die in your sins; if you do not believe that I am he, you will indeed die in your sins.'

²⁵ 'Who are you?' they asked.

'Just what I have been telling you from the beginning,' Jesus replied. ²⁶ 'I have much to say in judgment of you. But he who sent me is trustworthy, and what I have heard from him I tell the world.'

²⁷ They did not understand that he was telling them about his Father. ²⁸ So Jesus said, 'When you have lifted up the Son of Man, then you will know that I am he and that I do nothing on my own but speak just what the Father has taught me. ²⁹ The one who sent me is with me; he has not left me alone, for I always do what pleases him.' ³⁰ Even as he spoke, many believed in him.

Dispute over whose children Jesus' opponents are

³¹ To the Jews who had believed him, Jesus said, 'If you hold to my teaching, you are really my disciples. ³² Then you will know the truth, and the truth will set you free.'

[33] They answered him, 'We are Abraham's descendants and have never been slaves of anyone. How can you say that we shall be set free?'

[34] Jesus replied, 'Very truly I tell you, everyone who sins is a slave to sin. [35] Now a slave has no permanent place in the family, but a son belongs to it for ever. [36] So if the Son sets you free, you will be free indeed. [37] I know you are Abraham's descendants. Yet you are looking for a way to kill me, because you have no room for my word. [38] I am telling you what I have seen in the Father's presence, and you are doing what you have heard from your father.'

[39] 'Abraham is our father,' they answered.

'If you were Abraham's children,' said Jesus, 'then you would do what Abraham did. [40] As it is, you are looking for a way to kill me, a man who has told you the truth that I heard from God. Abraham did not do such things. [41] You are doing the works of your own father.'

'We are not illegitimate children,' they protested. 'The only Father we have is God himself.'

[42] Jesus said to them, 'If God were your Father, you would love me, for I have come here from God. I have not come on my own; God sent me. [43] Why is my language not clear to you? Because you are unable to hear what I say. [44] You belong to your father, the devil, and you want to carry out your father's desires. He was a murderer from the beginning, not holding to the truth, for there is no truth in him. When he lies, he speaks his native language, for he is a liar and the father of lies. [45] Yet because I tell the truth, you do not believe me! [46] Can any of you prove me guilty of sin? If I am telling the truth, why don't you believe me? [47] Whoever belongs to God hears what God says. The reason you do not hear is that you do not belong to God.'

JOHN 8:34-36

Jesus offers freedom, but how are we
enslaved? For Jesus, sin is to be
trapped in living a lie about God +
ourselves.

Jesus' claims about himself

[48] The Jews answered him, 'Aren't we right in saying that you are a Samaritan and demon-possessed?'

[49] 'I am not possessed by a demon,' said Jesus, 'but I honour my Father and you dishonour me. [50] I am not seeking glory for myself; but there is one who seeks it, and he is the judge. [51] Very truly I tell you, whoever obeys my word will never see death.'

[52] At this they exclaimed, 'Now we know that you are demon-possessed! Abraham died and so did the prophets, yet you say that whoever obeys your word will never taste death. [53] Are you greater than our father Abraham? He died, and so did the prophets. Who do you think you are?'

[54] Jesus replied, 'If I glorify myself, my glory means nothing. My Father, whom you claim as your God, is the one who glorifies me. [55] Though you do not know him, I know him. If I said I did not, I would be a liar like you, but I do know him and obey his word. [56] Your father Abraham rejoiced at the thought of seeing my day; he saw it and was glad.'

[57] 'You are not yet fifty years old,' they said to him, 'and you have seen Abraham!'

[58] 'Very truly I tell you,' Jesus answered, 'before Abraham was born, I am!' [59] At this, they picked up stones to stone him, but Jesus hid himself, slipping away from the temple grounds.

Jesus heals a man born blind

9 As he went along, he saw a man blind from birth. [2] His disciples asked him, 'Rabbi, who sinned, this man or his parents, that he was born blind?'

[3] 'Neither this man nor his parents sinned,' said Jesus, 'but this happened so that the works of God might be displayed in him. [4] As long as it is day, we must do the works

Cc
STUDY

BLIND FAITH

According to biologist Richard Dawkins,
'Faith is the great cop-out, the great excuse to
evade the need to think and evaluate evidence.
Faith is belief in spite of, even perhaps because
of, the lack of evidence.'

Do you agree that Christians believe without evidence? Is the Christian faith irrational?

STUDY: JOHN 9: 1-41 (PAGE 138)

WATCH: uncover.org.uk/john/video C

of him who sent me. Night is coming, when no one can work. [5] While I am in the world, I am the light of the world.'

[6] After saying this, he spat on the ground, made some mud with the saliva, and put it on the man's eyes. [7] 'Go,' he told him, 'wash in the Pool of Siloam' (this word means 'Sent'). So the man went and washed, and came home seeing.

[8] His neighbours and those who had formerly seen him begging asked, 'Isn't this the same man who used to sit and beg?' [9] Some claimed that he was.

Others said, 'No, he only looks like him.'

But he himself insisted, 'I am the man.'

[10] 'How then were your eyes opened?' they asked.

[11] He replied, 'The man they call Jesus made some mud and put it on my eyes. He told me to go to Siloam and wash. So I went and washed, and then I could see.'

[12] 'Where is this man?' they asked him.

'I don't know,' he said.

The Pharisees investigate the healing

[13] They brought to the Pharisees the man who had been blind. [14] Now the day on which Jesus had made the mud and opened the man's eyes was a Sabbath. [15] Therefore the Pharisees also asked him how he had received his sight. 'He put mud on my eyes,' the man replied, 'and I washed, and now I see.'

[16] Some of the Pharisees said, 'This man is not from God, for he does not keep the Sabbath.'

But others asked, 'How can a sinner perform such signs?' So they were divided.

[17] Then they turned again to the blind man, 'What have you to say about him? It was your eyes he opened.'

The man replied, 'He is a prophet.'

[18] They still did not believe that he had been blind and had received his sight until they sent for the man's parents.

19 'Is this your son?' they asked. 'Is this the one you say was born blind? How is it that now he can see?'

20 'We know he is our son,' the parents answered, 'and we know he was born blind. 21 But how he can see now, or who opened his eyes, we don't know. Ask him. He is of age; he will speak for himself.' 22 His parents said this because they were afraid of the Jewish leaders, who already had decided that anyone who acknowledged that Jesus was the Messiah would be put out of the synagogue. 23 That was why his parents said, 'He is of age; ask him.'

24 A second time they summoned the man who had been blind. 'Give glory to God by telling the truth,' they said. 'We know this man is a sinner.'

25 He replied, 'Whether he is a sinner or not, I don't know. One thing I do know. I was blind but now I see!'

26 Then they asked him, 'What did he do to you? How did he open your eyes?'

27 He answered, 'I have told you already and you did not listen. Why do you want to hear it again? Do you want to become his disciples too?'

28 Then they hurled insults at him and said, 'You are this fellow's disciple! We are disciples of Moses! 29 We know that God spoke to Moses, but as for this fellow, we don't even know where he comes from.'

30 The man answered, 'Now that is remarkable! You don't know where he comes from, yet he opened my eyes. 31 We know that God does not listen to sinners. He listens to the godly person who does his will. 32 Nobody has ever heard of opening the eyes of a man born blind. 33 If this man were not from God, he could do nothing.'

34 To this they replied, 'You were steeped in sin at birth; how dare you lecture us!' And they threw him out.

Spiritual blindness

³⁵ Jesus heard that they had thrown him out, and when he found him, he said, 'Do you believe in the Son of Man?'

³⁶ 'Who is he, sir?' the man asked. 'Tell me so that I may believe in him.'

³⁷ Jesus said, 'You have now seen him; in fact, he is the one speaking with you.'

³⁸ Then the man said, 'Lord, I believe,' and he worshipped him.

³⁹ Jesus said, 'For judgment I have come into this world, so that the blind will see and those who see will become blind.'

⁴⁰ Some Pharisees who were with him heard him say this and asked, 'What? Are we blind too?'

⁴¹ Jesus said, 'If you were blind, you would not be guilty of sin; but now that you claim you can see, your guilt remains.

The good shepherd and his sheep

10 'Very truly I tell you Pharisees, anyone who does not enter the sheepfold by the gate, but climbs in by some other way, is a thief and a robber. ² The one who enters by the gate is the shepherd of the sheep. ³ The gatekeeper opens the gate for him, and the sheep listen to his voice. He calls his own sheep by name and leads them out. ⁴ When he has brought out all his own, he goes on ahead of them, and his sheep follow him because they know his voice. ⁵ But they will never follow a stranger; in fact, they will run away from him because they do not recognise a stranger's voice.' ⁶ Jesus used this figure of speech, but the Pharisees did not understand what he was telling them.

⁷ Therefore Jesus said again, 'Very truly I tell you, I am the gate for the sheep. ⁸ All who have come before me are thieves and robbers, but the sheep have not listened to them. ⁹ I am the gate; whoever enters through me will be saved. They will come in and go out, and find pasture. ¹⁰ The thief comes only

to steal and kill and destroy; I have come that they may have life, and have it to the full.

11 'I am the good shepherd. The good shepherd lays down his life for the sheep. 12 The hired hand is not the shepherd and does not own the sheep. So when he sees the wolf coming, he abandons the sheep and runs away. Then the wolf attacks the flock and scatters it. 13 The man runs away because he is a hired hand and cares nothing for the sheep.

14 'I am the good shepherd; I know my sheep and my sheep know me – 15 just as the Father knows me and I know the Father – and I lay down my life for the sheep. 16 I have other sheep that are not of this sheepfold. I must bring them also. They too will listen to my voice, and there shall be one flock and one shepherd. 17 The reason my Father loves me is that I lay down my life – only to take it up again. 18 No one takes it from me, but I lay it down of my own accord. I have authority to lay it down and authority to take it up again. This command I received from my Father.'

19 The Jews who heard these words were again divided. 20 Many of them said, 'He is demon-possessed and raving mad. Why listen to him?'

21 But others said, 'These are not the sayings of a man possessed by a demon. Can a demon open the eyes of the blind?'

Further conflict over Jesus' claims

22 Then came the Festival of Dedication at Jerusalem. It was winter, 23 and Jesus was in the temple courts walking in Solomon's Colonnade. 24 The Jews who were there gathered round him, saying, 'How long will you keep us in suspense? If you are the Messiah, tell us plainly.'

25 Jesus answered, 'I did tell you, but you do not believe. The works I do in my Father's name testify about me, 26 but you do not believe because you are not my sheep.

JOHN 10:11

Jesus claims to be the one who truly cares for his people. What do you make of Jesus' character so far?

27 My sheep listen to my voice; I know them, and they follow me. 28 I give them eternal life, and they shall never perish; no one will snatch them out of my hand. 29 My Father, who has given them to me, is greater than all; no one can snatch them out of my Father's hand. 30 I and the Father are one.'

31 Again his Jewish opponents picked up stones to stone him, 32 but Jesus said to them, 'I have shown you many good works from the Father. For which of these do you stone me?'

33 'We are not stoning you for any good work,' they replied, 'but for blasphemy, because you, a mere man, claim to be God.'

34 Jesus answered them, 'Is it not written in your Law, "I have said you are 'gods' "? 35 If he called them "gods", to whom the word of God came – and Scripture cannot be set aside – 36 what about the one whom the Father set apart as his very own and sent into the world? Why then do you accuse me of blasphemy because I said, "I am God's Son"? 37 Do not believe me unless I do the works of my Father. 38 But if I do them, even though you do not believe me, believe the works, that you may know and understand that the Father is in me, and I in the Father.' 39 Again they tried to seize him, but he escaped their grasp.

40 Then Jesus went back across the Jordan to the place where John had been baptising in the early days. There he stayed, 41 and many people came to him. They said, 'Though John never performed a sign, all that John said about this man was true.' 42 And in that place many believed in Jesus.

The death of Lazarus

11 Now a man named Lazarus was ill. He was from Bethany, the village of Mary and her sister Martha. 2 (This Mary, whose brother Lazarus now lay ill, was the same one who poured perfume on the Lord and wiped his feet with her hair.) 3 So the sisters sent word to Jesus, 'Lord, the one you love is ill.'

This session explores the painful topic of death.

Why do you think it is a subject that we so often avoid talking openly about?

4 When he heard this, Jesus said, 'This illness will not end in death. No, it is for God's glory so that God's Son may be glorified through it.' 5 Now Jesus loved Martha and her sister and Lazarus. 6 So when he heard that Lazarus was ill, he stayed where he was two more days, 7 and then he said to his disciples, 'Let us go back to Judea.'

8 'But Rabbi,' they said, 'a short while ago the Jews there tried to stone you, and yet you are going back?'

9 Jesus answered, 'Are there not twelve hours of daylight? Anyone who walks in the day-time will not stumble, for they see by this world's light. 10 It is when a person walks at night that they stumble, for they have no light.'

11 After he had said this, he went on to tell them, 'Our friend Lazarus has fallen asleep; but I am going there to wake him up.'

12 His disciples replied, 'Lord, if he sleeps, he will get better.' 13 Jesus had been speaking of his death, but his disciples thought he meant natural sleep.

14 So then he told them plainly, 'Lazarus is dead, 15 and for your sake I am glad I was not there, so that you may believe. But let us go to him.'

16 Then Thomas (also known as Didymus) said to the rest of the disciples, 'Let us also go, that we may die with him.'

Jesus comforts the sisters of Lazarus

17 On his arrival, Jesus found that Lazarus had already been in the tomb for four days. 18 Now Bethany was less than two miles from Jerusalem, 19 and many Jews had come to Martha and Mary to comfort them in the loss of their brother. 20 When Martha heard that Jesus was coming, she went out to meet him, but Mary stayed at home.

21 'Lord,' Martha said to Jesus, 'if you had been here, my brother would not have died. 22 But I know that even now God will give you whatever you ask.'

²³ Jesus said to her, 'Your brother will rise again.'

²⁴ Martha answered, 'I know he will rise again in the resurrection at the last day.'

²⁵ Jesus said to her, 'I am the resurrection and the life. The one who believes in me will live, even though they die; ²⁶ and whoever lives by believing in me will never die. Do you believe this?'

²⁷ 'Yes, Lord,' she replied, 'I believe that you are the Messiah, the Son of God, who is to come into the world.'

²⁸ After she had said this, she went back and called her sister Mary aside. 'The Teacher is here,' she said, 'and is asking for you.' ²⁹ When Mary heard this, she got up quickly and went to him. ³⁰ Now Jesus had not yet entered the village, but was still at the place where Martha had met him. ³¹ When the Jews who had been with Mary in the house, comforting her, noticed how quickly she got up and went out, they followed her, supposing she was going to the tomb to mourn there.

³² When Mary reached the place where Jesus was and saw him, she fell at his feet and said, 'Lord, if you had been here, my brother would not have died.'

³³ When Jesus saw her weeping, and the Jews who had come along with her also weeping, he was deeply moved in spirit and troubled. ³⁴ 'Where have you laid him?' he asked.

'Come and see, Lord,' they replied.

³⁵ Jesus wept.

³⁶ Then the Jews said, 'See how he loved him!'

³⁷ But some of them said, 'Could not he who opened the eyes of the blind man have kept this man from dying?'

Jesus raises Lazarus from the dead

³⁸ Jesus, once more deeply moved, came to the tomb. It was a cave with a stone laid across the entrance. ³⁹ 'Take away the stone,' he said.

'But, Lord,' said Martha, the sister of the dead man, 'by this time there is a bad odour, for he has been there four days.'

⁴⁰ Then Jesus said, 'Did I not tell you that if you believe, you will see the glory of God?'

⁴¹ So they took away the stone. Then Jesus looked up and said, 'Father, I thank you that you have heard me. ⁴² I knew that you always hear me, but I said this for the benefit of the people standing here, that they may believe that you sent me.'

⁴³ When he had said this, Jesus called in a loud voice, 'Lazarus, come out!' ⁴⁴ The dead man came out, his hands and feet wrapped with strips of linen, and a cloth round his face.

Jesus said to them, 'Take off the grave clothes and let him go.'

The plot to kill Jesus

⁴⁵ Therefore many of the Jews who had come to visit Mary, and had seen what Jesus did, believed in him. ⁴⁶ But some of them went to the Pharisees and told them what Jesus had done. ⁴⁷ Then the chief priests and the Pharisees called a meeting of the Sanhedrin.

'What are we accomplishing?' they asked. 'Here is this man performing many signs. ⁴⁸ If we let him go on like this, everyone will believe in him, and then the Romans will come and take away both our temple and our nation.'

⁴⁹ Then one of them, named Caiaphas, who was high priest that year, spoke up, 'You know nothing at all! ⁵⁰ You do not realise that it is better for you that one man die for the people than that the whole nation perish.'

⁵¹ He did not say this on his own, but as high priest that year he prophesied that Jesus would die for the Jewish nation, ⁵² and not only for that nation but also for the scattered children of God, to bring them together and make them one. ⁵³ So from that day on they plotted to take his life.

⁵⁴ Therefore Jesus no longer moved about publicly among the people of Judea. Instead he withdrew to a region near the wilderness, to a village called Ephraim, where he stayed with his disciples.

⁵⁵ When it was almost time for the Jewish Passover, many went up from the country to Jerusalem for their ceremonial cleansing before the Passover. ⁵⁶ They kept looking for Jesus, and as they stood in the temple courts they asked one another, 'What do you think? Isn't he coming to the festival at all?' ⁵⁷ But the chief priests and the Pharisees had given orders that anyone who found out where Jesus was should report it so that they might arrest him.

Jesus anointed at Bethany

12 Six days before the Passover, Jesus came to Bethany, where Lazarus lived, whom Jesus had raised from the dead. ² Here a dinner was given in Jesus' honour. Martha served, while Lazarus was among those reclining at the table with him. ³ Then Mary took about half a litre of pure nard, an expensive perfume; she poured it on Jesus' feet and wiped his feet with her hair. And the house was filled with the fragrance of the perfume.

⁴ But one of his disciples, Judas Iscariot, who was later to betray him, objected, ⁵ 'Why wasn't this perfume sold and the money given to the poor? It was worth a year's wages.' ⁶ He did not say this because he cared about the poor but because he was a thief; as keeper of the money bag, he used to help himself to what was put into it.

⁷ 'Leave her alone,' Jesus replied. 'It was intended that she should save this perfume for the day of my burial. ⁸ You will always have the poor among you, but you will not always have me.'

⁹ Meanwhile a large crowd of Jews found out that Jesus was there and came, not only because of him but also to see

Lazarus, whom he had raised from the dead. [10] So the chief priests made plans to kill Lazarus as well, [11] for on account of him many of the Jews were going over to Jesus and believing in him.

Jesus comes to Jerusalem as king

[12] The next day the great crowd that had come for the festival heard that Jesus was on his way to Jerusalem. [13] They took palm branches and went out to meet him, shouting,

'Hosanna!'

'Blessed is he who comes in the name of the Lord!'

'Blessed is the king of Israel!'

[14] Jesus found a young donkey and sat upon it, as it is written:

[15] 'Do not be afraid, Daughter Zion;
    see, your king is coming,
    seated on a donkey's colt.'

[16] At first his disciples did not understand all this. Only after Jesus was glorified did they realise that these things had been written about him and that these things had been done to him.

[17] Now the crowd that was with him when he called Lazarus from the tomb and raised him from the dead continued to spread the word. [18] Many people, because they had heard that he had performed this sign, went out to meet him. [19] So the Pharisees said to one another, 'See, this is getting us nowhere. Look how the whole world has gone after him!'

Jesus predicts his death

[20] Now there were some Greeks among those who went up to worship at the festival. [21] They came to Philip, who was from Bethsaida in Galilee, with a request. 'Sir,' they said, 'we

JOHN 12:13

The crowds see Jesus as the one
who will fulfil the ancient promises
of a king who will liberate his people.
Have they got Jesus right?

would like to see Jesus.' [22] Philip went to tell Andrew; Andrew and Philip in turn told Jesus.

[23] Jesus replied, 'The hour has come for the Son of Man to be glorified. [24] Very truly I tell you, unless a grain of wheat falls to the ground and dies, it remains only a single seed. But if it dies, it produces many seeds. [25] Anyone who loves their life will lose it, while anyone who hates their life in this world will keep it for eternal life. [26] Whoever serves me must follow me; and where I am, my servant also will be. My Father will honour the one who serves me.

[27] 'Now my soul is troubled, and what shall I say? "Father, save me from this hour"? No, it was for this very reason I came to this hour. [28] Father, glorify your name!'

Then a voice came from heaven, 'I have glorified it, and will glorify it again.' [29] The crowd that was there and heard it said it had thundered; others said an angel had spoken to him.

[30] Jesus said, 'This voice was for your benefit, not mine. [31] Now is the time for judgment on this world; now the prince of this world will be driven out. [32] And I, when I am lifted up from the earth, will draw all people to myself.' [33] He said this to show the kind of death he was going to die.

[34] The crowd spoke up, 'We have heard from the Law that the Messiah will remain for ever, so how can you say, "The Son of Man must be lifted up"? Who is this "Son of Man"?'

[35] Then Jesus told them, 'You are going to have the light just a little while longer. Walk while you have the light, before darkness overtakes you. Whoever walks in the dark does not know where they are going. [36] Believe in the light while you have the light, so that you may become children of light.' When he had finished speaking, Jesus left and hid himself from them.

JOHN 12:27-28

At last Jesus' 'hour' has come —
a time, he says, for his glory.

JOHN 12:33

But now John tells us the hour
refers to his death — how can
Jesus' death lead to glory?

Belief and unbelief among the Jews

37 Even after Jesus had performed so many signs in their presence, they still would not believe in him. 38 This was to fulfil the word of Isaiah the prophet:

'Lord, who has believed our message
and to whom has the arm of the Lord been revealed?'

39 For this reason they could not believe, because, as Isaiah says elsewhere:

40 'He has blinded their eyes
and hardened their hearts,
so they can neither see with their eyes,
nor understand with their hearts,
nor turn – and I would heal them.'

41 Isaiah said this because he saw Jesus' glory and spoke about him.

42 Yet at the same time many even among the leaders believed in him. But because of the Pharisees they would not openly acknowledge their faith for fear they would be put out of the synagogue; 43 for they loved human praise more than praise from God.

44 Then Jesus cried out, 'Whoever believes in me does not believe in me only, but in the one who sent me. 45 The one who looks at me is seeing the one who sent me. 46 I have come into the world as a light, so that no one who believes in me should stay in darkness.

47 'If anyone hears my words but does not keep them, I do not judge that person. For I did not come to judge the world, but to save the world. 48 There is a judge for the one who rejects me and does not accept my words; the very words I have spoken will condemn them at the last day. 49 For I did not speak on my own, but the Father who sent me commanded me to say all that I have spoken. 50 I know that his command leads to eternal life. So whatever I say is just what the Father has told me to say.'

Jesus washes his disciples' feet

13 It was just before the Passover Festival. Jesus knew that the hour had come for him to leave this world and go to the Father. Having loved his own who were in the world, he loved them to the end.

2 The evening meal was in progress, and the devil had already prompted Judas, the son of Simon Iscariot, to betray Jesus. 3 Jesus knew that the Father had put all things under his power, and that he had come from God and was returning to God; 4 so he got up from the meal, took off his outer clothing, and wrapped a towel round his waist. 5 After that, he poured water into a basin and began to wash his disciples' feet, drying them with the towel that was wrapped round him.

6 He came to Simon Peter, who said to him, 'Lord, are you going to wash my feet?'

7 Jesus replied, 'You do not realise now what I am doing, but later you will understand.'

8 'No,' said Peter, 'you shall never wash my feet.'

Jesus answered, 'Unless I wash you, you have no part with me.'

9 'Then, Lord,' Simon Peter replied, 'not just my feet but my hands and my head as well!'

10 Jesus answered, 'Those who have had a bath need only to wash their feet; their whole body is clean. And you are clean, though not every one of you.' 11 For he knew who was going to betray him, and that was why he said not every one was clean.

12 When he had finished washing their feet, he put on his clothes and returned to his place. 'Do you understand what I have done for you?' he asked them. 13 'You call me "Teacher" and "Lord", and rightly so, for that is what I am. 14 Now that I, your Lord and Teacher, have washed your feet, you also should wash one another's feet. 15 I have set you an example

JOHN 13:14

Jesus' washing his disciples' feet
would have been culturally shocking.
Yet, he makes it the pattern for the
love his disciples should express.

that you should do as I have done for you. [16] Very truly I tell you, no servant is greater than his master, nor is a messenger greater than the one who sent him. [17] Now that you know these things, you will be blessed if you do them.

Jesus predicts his betrayal

[18] 'I am not referring to all of you; I know those I have chosen. But this is to fulfil this passage of Scripture: "He who shared my bread has turned against me."

[19] 'I am telling you now before it happens, so that when it does happen you will believe that I am who I am. [20] Very truly I tell you, whoever accepts anyone I send accepts me; and whoever accepts me accepts the one who sent me.'

[21] After he had said this, Jesus was troubled in spirit and testified, 'Very truly I tell you, one of you is going to betray me.'

[22] His disciples stared at one another, at a loss to know which of them he meant. [23] One of them, the disciple whom Jesus loved, was reclining next to him. [24] Simon Peter motioned to this disciple and said, 'Ask him which one he means.'

[25] Leaning back against Jesus, he asked him, 'Lord, who is it?'

[26] Jesus answered, 'It is the one to whom I will give this piece of bread when I have dipped it in the dish.' Then, dipping the piece of bread, he gave it to Judas, the son of Simon Iscariot. [27] As soon as Judas took the bread, Satan entered into him.

So Jesus told him, 'What you are about to do, do quickly.' [28] But no one at the meal understood why Jesus said this to him. [29] Since Judas had charge of the money, some thought Jesus was telling him to buy what was needed for the festival, or to give something to the poor. [30] As soon as Judas had taken the bread, he went out. And it was night.

Jesus predicts Peter's denial

31 When he was gone, Jesus said, 'Now the Son of Man is glorified and God is glorified in him. 32 If God is glorified in him, God will glorify the Son in himself, and will glorify him at once.

33 'My children, I will be with you only a little longer. You will look for me, and just as I told the Jews, so I tell you now: where I am going, you cannot come.

34 'A new command I give you: love one another. As I have loved you, so you must love one another. 35 By this everyone will know that you are my disciples, if you love one another.'

36 Simon Peter asked him, 'Lord, where are you going?'

Jesus replied, 'Where I am going, you cannot follow now, but you will follow later.'

37 Peter asked, 'Lord, why can't I follow you now? I will lay down my life for you.'

38 Then Jesus answered, 'Will you really lay down your life for me? Very truly I tell you, before the cock crows, you will disown me three times!

Jesus comforts his disciples

14 'Do not let your hearts be troubled. You believe in God; believe also in me. 2 My Father's house has many rooms; if that were not so, would I have told you that I am going there to prepare a place for you? 3 And if I go and prepare a place for you, I will come back and take you to be with me that you also may be where I am. 4 You know the way to the place where I am going.'

Jesus the way to the Father

5 Thomas said to him, 'Lord, we don't know where you are going, so how can we know the way?'

⁶ Jesus answered, 'I am the way and the truth and the life. No one comes to the Father except through me. ⁷ If you really know me, you will know my Father as well. From now on, you do know him and have seen him.'

⁸ Philip said, 'Lord, show us the Father and that will be enough for us.'

⁹ Jesus answered: 'Don't you know me, Philip, even after I have been among you such a long time? Anyone who has seen me has seen the Father. How can you say, "Show us the Father"? ¹⁰ Don't you believe that I am in the Father, and that the Father is in me? The words I say to you I do not speak on my own authority. Rather, it is the Father, living in me, who is doing his work. ¹¹ Believe me when I say that I am in the Father and the Father is in me; or at least believe on the evidence of the works themselves. ¹² Very truly I tell you, whoever believes in me will do the works I have been doing, and they will do even greater things than these, because I am going to the Father. ¹³ And I will do whatever you ask in my name, so that the Father may be glorified in the Son. ¹⁴ You may ask me for anything in my name, and I will do it.

Jesus promises the Holy Spirit

¹⁵ 'If you love me, keep my commands. ¹⁶ And I will ask the Father, and he will give you another advocate to help you and be with you for ever – ¹⁷ the Spirit of truth. The world cannot accept him, because it neither sees him nor knows him. But you know him, for he lives with you and will be in you. ¹⁸ I will not leave you as orphans; I will come to you. ¹⁹ Before long, the world will not see me any more, but you will see me. Because I live, you also will live. ²⁰ On that day you will realise that I am in my Father, and you are in me, and I am in you. ²¹ Whoever has my commands and keeps them is the one who loves me. The one who loves me will be loved by my Father, and I too will love them and show myself to them.'

JOHN 14:6

Jesus asserts that he is the only
way to God. At this point in the
Gospel, what do you make of
that claim?

²²Then Judas (not Judas Iscariot) said, 'But, Lord, why do you intend to show yourself to us and not to the world?'

²³Jesus replied, 'Anyone who loves me will obey my teaching. My Father will love them, and we will come to them and make our home with them. ²⁴Anyone who does not love me will not obey my teaching. These words you hear are not my own; they belong to the Father who sent me.

²⁵'All this I have spoken while still with you. ²⁶But the Advocate, the Holy Spirit, whom the Father will send in my name, will teach you all things and will remind you of everything I have said to you. ²⁷Peace I leave with you; my peace I give you. I do not give to you as the world gives. Do not let your hearts be troubled and do not be afraid.

²⁸'You heard me say, "I am going away and I am coming back to you." If you loved me, you would be glad that I am going to the Father, for the Father is greater than I. ²⁹I have told you now before it happens, so that when it does happen you will believe. ³⁰I will not say much more to you, for the prince of this world is coming. He has no hold over me, ³¹but he comes so that the world may learn that I love the Father and do exactly what my Father has commanded me.

'Come now; let us leave.

The vine and the branches

15 'I am the true vine, and my Father is the gardener. ²He cuts off every branch in me that bears no fruit, while every branch that does bear fruit he prunes so that it will be even more fruitful. ³You are already clean because of the word I have spoken to you. ⁴Remain in me, as I also remain in you. No branch can bear fruit by itself; it must remain in the vine. Neither can you bear fruit unless you remain in me.

5 'I am the vine; you are the branches. If you remain in me and I in you, you will bear much fruit; apart from me you can do nothing. 6 If you do not remain in me, you are like a branch that is thrown away and withers; such branches are picked up, thrown into the fire and burned. 7 If you remain in me and my words remain in you, ask whatever you wish, and it will be done for you. 8 This is to my Father's glory, that you bear much fruit, showing yourselves to be my disciples.

9 'As the Father has loved me, so have I loved you. Now remain in my love. 10 If you keep my commands, you will remain in my love, just as I have kept my Father's commands and remain in his love. 11 I have told you this so that my joy may be in you and that your joy may be complete. 12 My command is this: love each other as I have loved you. 13 Greater love has no one than this: to lay down one's life for one's friends. 14 You are my friends if you do what I command. 15 I no longer call you servants, because a servant does not know his master's business. Instead, I have called you friends, for everything that I learned from my Father I have made known to you. 16 You did not choose me, but I chose you and appointed you so that you might go and bear fruit – fruit that will last – and so that whatever you ask in my name the Father will give you. 17 This is my command: love each other.

The world hates the disciples

18 'If the world hates you, keep in mind that it hated me first. 19 If you belonged to the world, it would love you as its own. As it is, you do not belong to the world, but I have chosen you out of the world. That is why the world hates you. 20 Remember what I told you: "A servant is not greater than his master." If they persecuted me, they will persecute you also. If they obeyed my teaching, they will obey yours also.

JOHN 15:18

Jesus predicts that people will hate
his followers. If that's true, why
would anyone choose to follow
Jesus?

21 They will treat you this way because of my name, for they do not know the one who sent me. 22 If I had not come and spoken to them, they would not be guilty of sin; but now they have no excuse for their sin. 23 Whoever hates me hates my Father as well. 24 If I had not done among them the works no one else did, they would not be guilty of sin. As it is, they have seen, and yet they have hated both me and my Father. 25 But this is to fulfil what is written in their Law: "They hated me without reason."

The work of the Holy Spirit

26 'When the Advocate comes, whom I will send to you from the Father – the Spirit of truth who goes out from the Father – he will testify about me. 27 And you also must testify, for you have been with me from the beginning.

16 'All this I have told you so that you will not fall away. 2 They will put you out of the synagogue; in fact, the time is coming when anyone who kills you will think they are offering a service to God. 3 They will do such things because they have not known the Father or me. 4 I have told you this, so that when their time comes you will remember that I warned you about them. I did not tell you this from the beginning because I was with you, 5 but now I am going to him who sent me. None of you asks me, "Where are you going?" 6 Rather, you are filled with grief because I have said these things. 7 But very truly I tell you, it is for your good that I am going away. Unless I go away, the Advocate will not come to you; but if I go, I will send him to you. 8 When he comes, he will prove the world to be in the wrong about sin and righteousness and judgment: 9 about sin, because people do not believe in me; 10 about righteousness, because I am going to the Father, where you can see me no longer; 11 and about judgment, because the prince of this world now stands condemned.

¹²'I have much more to say to you, more than you can now bear. ¹³But when he, the Spirit of truth, comes, he will guide you into all the truth. He will not speak on his own; he will speak only what he hears, and he will tell you what is yet to come. ¹⁴He will glorify me because it is from me that he will receive what he will make known to you. ¹⁵All that belongs to the Father is mine. That is why I said the Spirit will receive from me what he will make known to you.'

The disciples' grief will turn to joy

¹⁶Jesus went on to say, 'In a little while you will see me no more, and then after a little while you will see me.'

¹⁷At this, some of his disciples said to one another, 'What does he mean by saying, "In a little while you will see me no more, and then after a little while you will see me," and "Because I am going to the Father"?' ¹⁸They kept asking, 'What does he mean by "a little while"? We don't understand what he is saying.'

¹⁹Jesus saw that they wanted to ask him about this, so he said to them, 'Are you asking one another what I meant when I said, "In a little while you will see me no more, and then after a little while you will see me"? ²⁰Very truly I tell you, you will weep and mourn while the world rejoices. You will grieve, but your grief will turn to joy. ²¹A woman giving birth to a child has pain because her time has come; but when her baby is born she forgets the anguish because of her joy that a child is born into the world. ²²So with you: now is your time of grief, but I will see you again and you will rejoice, and no one will take away your joy. ²³In that day you will no longer ask me anything. Very truly I tell you, my Father will give you whatever you ask in my name. ²⁴Until now you have not asked for anything in my name. Ask and you will receive, and your joy will be complete.

25 'Though I have been speaking figuratively, a time is coming when I will no longer use this kind of language but will tell you plainly about my Father. 26 In that day you will ask in my name. I am not saying that I will ask the Father on your behalf. 27 No, the Father himself loves you because you have loved me and have believed that I came from God. 28 I came from the Father and entered the world; now I am leaving the world and going back to the Father.'

29 Then Jesus' disciples said, 'Now you are speaking clearly and without figures of speech. 30 Now we can see that you know all things and that you do not even need to have anyone ask you questions. This makes us believe that you came from God.'

31 'Do you now believe?' Jesus replied. 32 'A time is coming and in fact has come when you will be scattered, each to your own home. You will leave me all alone. Yet I am not alone, for my Father is with me.

33 'I have told you these things, so that in me you may have peace. In this world you will have trouble. But take heart! I have overcome the world.'

Jesus prays to be glorified

17 After Jesus said this, he looked towards heaven and prayed:

'Father, the hour has come. Glorify your Son, that your Son may glorify you. 2 For you granted him authority over all people that he might give eternal life to all those you have given him. 3 Now this is eternal life: that they know you, the only true God, and Jesus Christ, whom you have sent. 4 I have brought you glory on earth by finishing the work you gave me to do. 5 And now, Father, glorify me in your presence with the glory I had with you before the world began.

JOHN 17:3

Jesus defines eternal life as knowing
the Father + knowing Him. Does
that definition surprise you? Do
you find it attractive?

Jesus prays for his disciples

⁶ 'I have revealed you to those whom you gave me out of the world. They were yours; you gave them to me and they have obeyed your word. ⁷ Now they know that everything you have given me comes from you. ⁸ For I gave them the words you gave me and they accepted them. They knew with certainty that I came from you, and they believed that you sent me. ⁹ I pray for them. I am not praying for the world, but for those you have given me, for they are yours. ¹⁰ All I have is yours, and all you have is mine. And glory has come to me through them. ¹¹ I will remain in the world no longer, but they are still in the world, and I am coming to you. Holy Father, protect them by the power of your name, the name you gave me, so that they may be one as we are one. ¹² While I was with them, I protected them and kept them safe by that name you gave me. None has been lost except the one doomed to destruction so that Scripture would be fulfilled.

¹³ 'I am coming to you now, but I say these things while I am still in the world, so that they may have the full measure of my joy within them. ¹⁴ I have given them your word and the world has hated them, for they are not of the world any more than I am of the world. ¹⁵ My prayer is not that you take them out of the world but that you protect them from the evil one. ¹⁶ They are not of the world, even as I am not of it. ¹⁷ Sanctify them by the truth; your word is truth. ¹⁸ As you sent me into the world, I have sent them into the world. ¹⁹ For them I sanctify myself, that they too may be truly sanctified.

Jesus prays for all believers

²⁰ 'My prayer is not for them alone. I pray also for those who will believe in me through their message, ²¹ that all of them may be one, Father, just as you are in me and I am in

you. May they also be in us so that the world may believe that you have sent me. ²²I have given them the glory that you gave me, that they may be one as we are one – ²³I in them and you in me – so that they may be brought to complete unity. Then the world will know that you sent me and have loved them even as you have loved me.

²⁴'Father, I want those you have given me to be with me where I am, and to see my glory, the glory you have given me because you loved me before the creation of the world.

²⁵'Righteous Father, though the world does not know you, I know you, and they know that you have sent me. ²⁶I have made you known to them, and will continue to make you known in order that the love you have for me may be in them and that I myself may be in them.'

Jesus arrested

18 When he had finished praying, Jesus left with his disciples and crossed the Kidron Valley. On the other side there was a garden, and he and his disciples went into it.

²Now Judas, who betrayed him, knew the place, because Jesus had often met there with his disciples. ³So Judas came to the garden, guiding a detachment of soldiers and some officials from the chief priests and the Pharisees. They were carrying torches, lanterns and weapons.

⁴Jesus, knowing all that was going to happen to him, went out and asked them, 'Who is it you want?'

⁵'Jesus of Nazareth,' they replied.

'I am he,' Jesus said. (And Judas the traitor was standing there with them.) ⁶When Jesus said, 'I am he,' they drew back and fell to the ground.

⁷Again he asked them, 'Who is it you want?'

'Jesus of Nazareth,' they said.

⁸Jesus answered, 'I told you that I am he. If you are looking for me, then let these men go.' ⁹This happened so

JOHN 18:6

God had called himself "I AM
WHO I AM" in the Hebrew Scriptures.
As Jesus uses that name, he floors
a detachment of 200 soldiers.

that the words he had spoken would be fulfilled: 'I have not lost one of those you gave me.'

¹⁰ Then Simon Peter, who had a sword, drew it and struck the high priest's servant, cutting off his right ear. (The servant's name was Malchus.)

¹¹ Jesus commanded Peter, 'Put your sword away! Shall I not drink the cup the Father has given me?'

¹² Then the detachment of soldiers with its commander and the Jewish officials arrested Jesus. They bound him ¹³ and brought him first to Annas, who was the father-in-law of Caiaphas, the high priest that year. ¹⁴ Caiaphas was the one who had advised the Jewish leaders that it would be good if one man died for the people.

Peter's first denial

¹⁵ Simon Peter and another disciple were following Jesus. Because this disciple was known to the high priest, he went with Jesus into the high priest's courtyard, ¹⁶ but Peter had to wait outside at the door. The other disciple, who was known to the high priest, came back, spoke to the servant-girl on duty there and brought Peter in.

¹⁷ 'You aren't one of this man's disciples too, are you?' she asked Peter.

He replied, 'I am not.'

¹⁸ It was cold, and the servants and officials stood round a fire they had made to keep warm. Peter also was standing with them, warming himself.

The high priest questions Jesus

¹⁹ Meanwhile, the high priest questioned Jesus about his disciples and his teaching.

²⁰ 'I have spoken openly to the world,' Jesus replied. 'I always taught in synagogues or at the temple, where all the Jews come together. I said nothing in secret. ²¹ Why question me? Ask those who heard me. Surely they know what I said.'

²²When Jesus said this, one of the officials near by slapped him in the face. 'Is this the way you answer the high priest?' he demanded.

²³'If I said something wrong,' Jesus replied, 'testify as to what is wrong. But if I spoke the truth, why did you strike me?' ²⁴Then Annas sent him bound to Caiaphas the high priest.

Peter's second and third denials

²⁵Meanwhile, Simon Peter was still standing there warming himself. So they asked him, 'You aren't one of his disciples too, are you?'

He denied it, saying, 'I am not.'

²⁶One of the high priest's servants, a relative of the man whose ear Peter had cut off, challenged him, 'Didn't I see you with him in the garden?' ²⁷Again Peter denied it, and at that moment a cock began to crow.

Jesus before Pilate

²⁸Then the Jewish leaders took Jesus from Caiaphas to the palace of the Roman governor. By now it was early morning, and to avoid ceremonial uncleanness they did not enter the palace, because they wanted to be able to eat the Passover. ²⁹So Pilate came out to them and asked, 'What charges are you bringing against this man?'

³⁰'If he were not a criminal,' they replied, 'we would not have handed him over to you.'

³¹Pilate said, 'Take him yourselves and judge him by your own law.'

'But we have no right to execute anyone,' they objected. ³²This took place to fulfil what Jesus had said about the kind of death he was going to die.

³³Pilate then went back inside the palace, summoned Jesus and asked him, 'Are you the king of the Jews?'

JOHN 18:23

While Peter denies him, Jesus stands firm under questioning. Why do you think the authorities are so eager to condemn Jesus?

³⁴'Is that your own idea,' Jesus asked, 'or did others talk to you about me?'

³⁵'Am I a Jew?' Pilate replied. 'Your own people and chief priests handed you over to me. What is it you have done?'

³⁶Jesus said, 'My kingdom is not of this world. If it were, my servants would fight to prevent my arrest by the Jewish leaders. But now my kingdom is from another place.'

³⁷'You are a king, then!' said Pilate.

Jesus answered, 'You say that I am a king. In fact, the reason I was born and came into the world is to testify to the truth. Everyone on the side of truth listens to me.'

³⁸'What is truth?' retorted Pilate. With this he went out again to the Jews gathered there and said, 'I find no basis for a charge against him. ³⁹But it is your custom for me to release to you one prisoner at the time of the Passover. Do you want me to release "the king of the Jews"?'

⁴⁰They shouted back, 'No, not him! Give us Barabbas!' Now Barabbas had taken part in an uprising.

Jesus sentenced to be crucified

19 Then Pilate took Jesus and had him flogged. ²The soldiers twisted together a crown of thorns and put it on his head. They clothed him in a purple robe ³and went up to him again and again, saying, 'Hail, king of the Jews!' And they slapped him in the face.

⁴Once more Pilate came out and said to the Jews gathered there, 'Look, I am bringing him out to you to let you know that I find no basis for a charge against him.' ⁵When Jesus came out wearing the crown of thorns and the purple robe, Pilate said to them, 'Here is the man!'

⁶As soon as the chief priests and their officials saw him, they shouted, 'Crucify! Crucify!'

But Pilate answered, 'You take him and crucify him. As for me, I find no basis for a charge against him.'

Russian novelist and human rights campaigner Alexander Solzhenitsyn considered the hypothetical possibility of ridding the world of evil people. He eventually came to the conclusion that this would be impossible: 'The line dividing good and evil cuts through the heart of every human being. And who is willing to destroy a piece of his own heart?'

To what extent do you agree with this description of humanity?

STUDY: JOHN 19: 1-42 (PAGE 150)

WATCH: uncover.org.uk/john/video E

7 The Jewish leaders insisted, 'We have a law, and according to that law he must die, because he claimed to be the Son of God.'

8 When Pilate heard this, he was even more afraid, 9 and he went back inside the palace. 'Where do you come from?' he asked Jesus, but Jesus gave him no answer. 10 'Do you refuse to speak to me?' Pilate said. 'Don't you realise I have power either to free you or to crucify you?'

11 Jesus answered, 'You would have no power over me if it were not given to you from above. Therefore the one who handed me over to you is guilty of a greater sin.'

12 From then on, Pilate tried to set Jesus free, but the Jewish leaders kept shouting, 'If you let this man go, you are no friend of Caesar. Anyone who claims to be a king opposes Caesar.'

13 When Pilate heard this, he brought Jesus out and sat down on the judge's seat at a place known as the Stone Pavement (which in Aramaic is Gabbatha). 14 It was the day of Preparation of the Passover; it was about noon.

'Here is your king,' Pilate said to the Jews.

15 But they shouted, 'Take him away! Take him away! Crucify him!'

'Shall I crucify your king?' Pilate asked.

'We have no king but Caesar,' the chief priests answered.

16 Finally Pilate handed him over to them to be crucified.

The crucifixion of Jesus

So the soldiers took charge of Jesus. 17 Carrying his own cross, he went out to the place of the Skull (which in Aramaic is called Golgotha). 18 There they crucified him, and with him two others – one on each side and Jesus in the middle.

19 Pilate had a notice prepared and fastened to the cross. It read: JESUS OF NAZARETH, THE KING OF THE JEWS. 20 Many of the Jews read this sign, for the place where Jesus was

crucified was near the city, and the sign was written in Aramaic, Latin and Greek. ²¹ The chief priests of the Jews protested to Pilate, 'Do not write "The King of the Jews", but that this man claimed to be king of the Jews.'

²² Pilate answered, 'What I have written, I have written.'

²³ When the soldiers crucified Jesus, they took his clothes, dividing them into four shares, one for each of them, with the undergarment remaining. This garment was seamless, woven in one piece from top to bottom.

²⁴ 'Let's not tear it,' they said to one another. 'Let's decide by lot who will get it.'

This happened that the scripture might be fulfilled that said,

'They divided my clothes among them
    and cast lots for my garment.'

So this is what the soldiers did.

²⁵ Near the cross of Jesus stood his mother, his mother's sister, Mary the wife of Clopas, and Mary Magdalene. ²⁶ When Jesus saw his mother there, and the disciple whom he loved standing near by, he said to her, 'Woman, here is your son,' ²⁷ and to the disciple, 'Here is your mother.' From that time on, this disciple took her into his home.

The death of Jesus

²⁸ Later, knowing that everything had now been finished, and so that Scripture would be fulfilled, Jesus said, 'I am thirsty.' ²⁹ A jar of wine vinegar was there, so they soaked a sponge in it, put the sponge on a stalk of the hyssop plant, and lifted it to Jesus' lips. ³⁰ When he had received the drink, Jesus said, 'It is finished.' With that, he bowed his head and gave up his spirit.

³¹ Now it was the day of Preparation, and the next day was to be a special Sabbath. Because the Jewish leaders did not want the bodies left on the crosses during the Sabbath, they asked Pilate to have the legs broken and the bodies taken down. ³² The soldiers therefore came and broke the legs of the first man who had been crucified with Jesus, and then those of the other. ³³ But when they came to Jesus and found that he was already dead, they did not break his legs. ³⁴ Instead, one of the soldiers pierced Jesus' side with a spear, bringing a sudden flow of blood and water. ³⁵ The man who saw it has given testimony, and his testimony is true. He knows that he tells the truth, and he testifies so that you also may believe. ³⁶ These things happened so that the scripture would be fulfilled: 'Not one of his bones will be broken,' ³⁷ and, as another scripture says, 'They will look on the one they have pierced.'

The burial of Jesus

³⁸ Later, Joseph of Arimathea asked Pilate for the body of Jesus. Now Joseph was a disciple of Jesus, but secretly because he feared the Jewish leaders. With Pilate's permission, he came and took the body away. ³⁹ He was accompanied by Nicodemus, the man who earlier had visited Jesus at night. Nicodemus brought a mixture of myrrh and aloes, about thirty-five kilograms. ⁴⁰ Taking Jesus' body, the two of them wrapped it, with the spices, in strips of linen. This was in accordance with Jewish burial customs. ⁴¹ At the place where Jesus was crucified, there was a garden, and in the garden a new tomb, in which no one had ever been laid. ⁴² Because it was the Jewish day of Preparation and since the tomb was near by, they laid Jesus there.

The empty tomb

20 Early on the first day of the week, while it was still dark, Mary Magdalene went to the tomb and saw that the stone had been removed from the entrance. ²So she came running to Simon Peter and the other disciple, the one Jesus loved, and said, 'They have taken the Lord out of the tomb, and we don't know where they have put him!'

³So Peter and the other disciple started for the tomb. ⁴Both were running, but the other disciple outran Peter and reached the tomb first. ⁵He bent over and looked in at the strips of linen lying there but did not go in. ⁶Then Simon Peter came along behind him and went straight into the tomb. He saw the strips of linen lying there, ⁷as well as the cloth that had been wrapped round Jesus' head. The cloth was still lying in its place, separate from the linen. ⁸Finally the other disciple, who had reached the tomb first, also went inside. He saw and believed. ⁹(They still did not understand from Scripture that Jesus had to rise from the dead.) ¹⁰Then the disciples went back to where they were staying.

Jesus appears to Mary Magdalene

¹¹Now Mary stood outside the tomb crying. As she wept, she bent over to look into the tomb ¹²and saw two angels in white, seated where Jesus' body had been, one at the head and the other at the foot.

¹³They asked her, 'Woman, why are you crying?'

'They have taken my Lord away,' she said, 'and I don't know where they have put him.' ¹⁴At this, she turned round and saw Jesus standing there, but she did not realise that it was Jesus.

¹⁵He asked her, 'Woman, why are you crying? Who is it you are looking for?'

Thinking he was the gardener, she said, 'Sir, if you have carried him away, tell me where you have put him, and I will get him.'

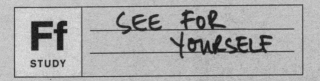

| **Ff** STUDY | SEE FOR YOURSELF |

Confirmation bias is the tendency to interpret new evidence as confirmation of one's existing beliefs or theories. Why do you think people can sometimes be resistant to questioning and changing their existing beliefs?

What kind of evidence would you need in order to change your mind about something?

| STUDY: | JOHN 20:1-29 (PAGE 156) |
| WATCH: | uncover.org.uk/john/video F |

¹⁶ Jesus said to her, 'Mary.'

She turned towards him and cried out in Aramaic, 'Rabboni!' (which means 'Teacher').

¹⁷ Jesus said, 'Do not hold on to me, for I have not yet ascended to the Father. Go instead to my brothers and tell them, "I am ascending to my Father and your Father, to my God and your God."'

¹⁸ Mary Magdalene went to the disciples with the news: 'I have seen the Lord!' And she told them that he had said these things to her.

Jesus appears to his disciples

¹⁹ On the evening of that first day of the week, when the disciples were together, with the doors locked for fear of the Jewish leaders, Jesus came and stood among them and said, 'Peace be with you!' ²⁰ After he said this, he showed them his hands and side. The disciples were overjoyed when they saw the Lord.

²¹ Again Jesus said, 'Peace be with you! As the Father has sent me, I am sending you.' ²² And with that he breathed on them and said, 'Receive the Holy Spirit. ²³ If you forgive anyone's sins, their sins are forgiven; if you do not forgive them, they are not forgiven.'

Jesus appears to Thomas

²⁴ Now Thomas (also known as Didymus), one of the Twelve, was not with the disciples when Jesus came. ²⁵ So the other disciples told him, 'We have seen the Lord!'

But he said to them, 'Unless I see the nail marks in his hands and put my finger where the nails were, and put my hand into his side, I will not believe.'

²⁶ A week later his disciples were in the house again, and Thomas was with them. Though the doors were locked, Jesus came and stood among them and said, 'Peace be with you!'

27 Then he said to Thomas, 'Put your finger here; see my hands. Reach out your hand and put it into my side. Stop doubting and believe.'

28 Thomas said to him, 'My Lord and my God!'

29 Then Jesus told him, 'Because you have seen me, you have believed; blessed are those who have not seen and yet have believed.'

The purpose of John's gospel

30 Jesus performed many other signs in the presence of his disciples, which are not recorded in this book. 31 But these are written that you may believe that Jesus is the Messiah, the Son of God, and that by believing you may have life in his name.

Jesus and the miraculous catch of fish

21 Afterwards Jesus appeared again to his disciples, by the Sea of Galilee. It happened this way: 2 Simon Peter, Thomas (also known as Didymus), Nathanael from Cana in Galilee, the sons of Zebedee, and two other disciples were together. 3 'I'm going out to fish,' Simon Peter told them, and they said, 'We'll go with you.' So they went out and got into the boat, but that night they caught nothing.

4 Early in the morning, Jesus stood on the shore, but the disciples did not realise that it was Jesus.

5 He called out to them, 'Friends, haven't you any fish?'

'No,' they answered.

6 He said, 'Throw your net on the right side of the boat and you will find some.' When they did, they were unable to haul the net in because of the large number of fish.

7 Then the disciple whom Jesus loved said to Peter, 'It is the Lord!' As soon as Simon Peter heard him say, 'It is the Lord,' he wrapped his outer garment round him (for he had taken it off) and jumped into the water. 8 The other disciples followed

JOHN 20:31

John sums up his aim in writing.
Do you think he has achieved it?

in the boat, towing the net full of fish, for they were not far from shore, about a hundred metres. ⁹ When they landed, they saw a fire of burning coals there with fish on it, and some bread.

¹⁰ Jesus said to them, 'Bring some of the fish you have just caught.' ¹¹ So Simon Peter climbed back into the boat and dragged the net ashore. It was full of large fish, 153, but even with so many the net was not torn. ¹² Jesus said to them, 'Come and have breakfast.' None of the disciples dared ask him, 'Who are you?' They knew it was the Lord. ¹³ Jesus came, took the bread and gave it to them, and did the same with the fish. ¹⁴ This was now the third time Jesus appeared to his disciples after he was raised from the dead.

Jesus reinstates Peter

¹⁵ When they had finished eating, Jesus said to Simon Peter, 'Simon son of John, do you love me more than these?'

'Yes, Lord,' he said, 'you know that I love you.'

Jesus said, 'Feed my lambs.'

¹⁶ Again Jesus said, 'Simon son of John, do you love me?'

He answered, 'Yes, Lord, you know that I love you.'

Jesus said, 'Take care of my sheep.'

¹⁷ The third time he said to him, 'Simon son of John, do you love me?'

Peter was hurt because Jesus asked him the third time, 'Do you love me?' He said, 'Lord, you know all things; you know that I love you.'

Jesus said, 'Feed my sheep. ¹⁸ Very truly I tell you, when you were younger you dressed yourself and went where you wanted; but when you are old you will stretch out your hands, and someone else will dress you and lead you where you do not want to go.' ¹⁹ Jesus said this to indicate the kind of death by which Peter would glorify God. Then he said to him, 'Follow me!'

JOHN 21:12

→ What kind of God cooks breakfast?
Is Jesus how you imagined him
to be? How does that shape your
view of God?

20 Peter turned and saw that the disciple whom Jesus loved was following them. (This was the one who had leaned back against Jesus at the supper and had said, 'Lord, who is going to betray you?') 21 When Peter saw him, he asked, 'Lord, what about him?'

22 Jesus answered, 'If I want him to remain alive until I return, what is that to you? You must follow me.' 23 Because of this, the rumour spread among the believers that this disciple would not die. But Jesus did not say that he would not die; he only said, 'If I want him to remain alive until I return, what is that to you?'

24 This is the disciple who testifies to these things and who wrote them down. We know that his testimony is true.

25 Jesus did many other things as well. If every one of them were written down, I suppose that even the whole world would not have room for the books that would be written.

→ <u>JOHN 21:24</u>

John insists his account is true.
Would you agree?

At the end of his gospel, John tells us that he selected his material in order to help us understand who Jesus is and what he came to do: "But these are written that you may believe that Jesus is the Messiah, the Son of God, and that by believing you may have life in his name." - John 20:31

What do you make of Jesus? A great man? A religious reformer? Or something more? The essence of John's message is that Jesus is the one who can give us life, who can restore our relationship with God because he gave up his life in a harrowing crucifixion.

Jesus is risen from the dead and we can experience the life he offers today.

It may be that you have come to believe these things are true and you want to receive the life that Jesus offers. You can speak to God now using this simple prayer:

Dear Father,

I am sorry that I've spent so long looking for life in the wrong places. Thank you that Jesus died so that I could be forgiven. Thank you that he rose again and I can find life in him. Father, please forgive me now and welcome me into eternal life with you. Please fill me with your Spirit so that I can live with Jesus as my Lord and my God.

Amen

There may still be some things you are unsure of. If you haven't already done so, why not work through the six studies in this Appendix with a friend?

You can also find out more about Jesus online at uncover.org.uk/john.

Jn
URL

UNCOVER MORE ONLINE

uncover.org.uk/john

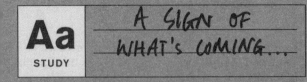

In his book *The Last Word*, author Thomas
Nagel writes, 'I want atheism to be true, and
I am made uneasy by the fact that some of
the most intelligent and well informed people
I know are religious believers. It isn't just that I
don't believe in God and, naturally, hope that
I'm right in my belief. It is that I hope there is
no God. I don't want there to be a God, I don't
want the universe to be like that.'

Why might someone 'hope there is no God'?

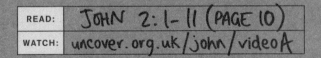

| READ: | JOHN 2: 1-11 (PAGE 10) |
| WATCH: | uncover.org.uk/john/videoA |

JOHN 20:30-31 (PAGE 118)

1 What reasons does John give for writing his biography of Jesus?

2 John makes the identity of Jesus a major theme of his book. Who do you think Jesus might have been? How did you come to this conclusion?

In ancient Jewish thought, the Christ or Messiah was a promised leader of the Jewish nation, who would defeat the nation's enemies and lead the people into an era of peace and prosperity.

HISTORICAL CONTEXT

The first public encounter that John presents us with is Jesus at a wedding with friends and family. Weddings in first-century Palestine were even more significant and lavish affairs than they are today. Marriage meant more than the joining of two individuals. A wedding marked the bride and groom's entrance into their community as adults. The celebrations usually lasted for at least a week. It was the responsibility of the groom to provide all that was necessary for such a hugely important social occasion.

JOHN 2: 1-11

3 The wedding has run out of wine. How might the bride and groom feel if there was no wine at their wedding feast, especially in a shame/honour culture?

4 If the wine was finished, what would the wedding crowd conclude about the groom in particular? What would the bride's family think about their new son-in-law?

In the Hebrew Bible, wine represented joy, so its absence at a wedding would be disastrous. Jesus' reply to his mother isn't as stark as it first looks, but it is quite puzzling, especially when he says, 'My hour has not yet come' in verse 4. Jesus seems to be a man who knows his destiny and sees his whole life as heading towards a particular moment.

5 Although Jesus is reluctant to step into the limelight at this point, why do you think he does something quite miraculous to help the couple?

6 Each of the six stone water jars would contain 80–120 litres, the equivalent of 700–1,000 bottles of wine. Describe the master of the banquet's impression of the wine. How will this wine change the party?

7 What does the master of the banquet conclude about the groom? Does the groom deserve the credit? How would the bride and groom feel about what Jesus has done for them?

8 The water jars contained water for ceremonial washing. Before each meal Jews would wash, as a symbol of washing away their sins before receiving what God had given them. Thus the water in the jars was a continual reminder of their guilt and need for cleansing. Given this background, what might be the significance of Jesus turning this water into the most beautiful wine?

Jesus quietly rescued a wedding and saved a desperate couple from disgrace. But his disciples (or followers) saw that his actions pointed to something far more significant about him. They would be familiar with ancient Hebrew texts such as the following from the prophet Isaiah (c.700 BC):

On this mountain the LORD Almighty will prepare
*   a feast of rich food for all peoples,*
a banquet of aged wine –
*   the best of meats and the finest of wines.*
On this mountain he will destroy
*   the shroud that enfolds all peoples,*
the sheet that covers all nations;
*   he will swallow up death for ever.*
The Sovereign LORD will wipe away the tears
*   from all faces;*
he will remove his people's disgrace
*   from all the earth (Isaiah 25:6–8).*

9 Isaiah imagines what it will be like when the Lord Almighty, God, comes to the world. What will God do, and for whom?

10 Imagine that you are one of Jesus' disciples. You have grown up in a Jewish household, with a text like this ringing in your ears. Having just tasted the new wine from Jesus, what might you think about him?

Isaiah is looking forward to a day when God himself will come to heal the world. Isaiah pictures this healing as the richest banquet imaginable. Other Hebrew texts speak about a particular person through whom God will do all this – the Messiah we were introduced to earlier. Could Jesus be the one who will fulfil all these hopes and dreams?

WHAT DOES THIS MEAN FOR US?

Some people hope there is no God because they perceive religion to be life-diminishing. Given what John has said about Jesus bringing life, what does this first encounter suggest about the life Jesus gives to those who believe in him? What does this suggest about who he is?

Bb
STUDY

'Resign yourself to the lifelong sadness that comes from never being satisfied.' Like many people, successful author Zadie Smith has found satisfaction elusive.

<u>Do you think it is possible to find lasting satisfaction, and, if so, how?</u>

READ:	JOHN 4:4-42 (PAGE 18)
WATCH:	uncover.org.uk/john/video B

HISTORICAL CONTEXT

In this encounter, Jesus does something that in his day would have been considered shocking. He speaks to a Samaritan woman. This might not sound like much, but in his culture, a religious man would never consider speaking to a woman in public. An ancient text said, 'Better is the wickedness of a man than a woman who does good; it is woman who brings shame and disgrace.' Jesus also ignores the deep racial and religious prejudice that Jews feel towards Samaritans. Jews consider Samaritans 'heretics' because they combine some Jewish teachings with pagan practices.

We join Jesus at noon (the sixth hour, as it was the custom to count the hour from sunrise), in the sweltering midday heat, when he is tired and thirsty.

JOHN 4:4-15

1   It was the custom for women to go together to the well to draw water in the cool of the morning. Why might this woman be drawing water alone and in the heat of the day?

2   Why is she so surprised that Jesus asks her for a drink?

3 How does Jesus describe the 'living water' he offers? What does Jesus mean when he uses the words 'thirst' and 'thirsty' in verse 13?

4 How do you think the woman is responding to what Jesus claims to offer? Is her request in verse 15 serious or cynical?

JOHN 4: 16-26

5 Jesus unexpectedly moves the conversation on to the subject of the woman's relationships. Why do you think she responds with less than the truth in verse 17?

6 How might her past relationships explain why she went to the well alone at noon and not with the other women in the morning?

7 Why do you think Jesus exposes the reality of her past relationships? How will this help her find living water and satisfaction for her thirst?

Unsettled by his insight into her life, the woman starts to recognise that Jesus is at the very least a prophet. Her comments in verse 20 are not a change of subject; rather, she is asking which temple she should go to in order to find forgiveness and be restored to God.

Jesus responds in verses 21-24 by saying that his coming into the world changes everything. People will no longer need to go somewhere to find forgiveness and worship God because his coming means people can know God personally and intimately, as 'Father' ('worship in the Spirit'). Nor will there be any confusion about where the truth lies because in his coming Jesus reveals the truth about God. Later in the Gospel Jesus describes himself as 'the truth'.

JOHN 4: 27-29, 39-42

8 Describe the reaction of the disciples when they return to the well in verse 27. Why do they react in this way?

9 Given all that we know about this woman, what strikes you as so surprising about her actions and words in verses 28–29? How do you think she feels now? Why?

10   According to verses 39–42, what do the people of the town come to believe, and what persuades them?

11   Reflecting on the whole encounter, what is the living water that Jesus claims to bring? If he is the 'Saviour of the world' what has he come to save people from?

WHAT DOES THIS MEAN FOR US?

Jesus locates our emptiness or 'thirst' in our alienation from God. He promises to bring us into an intimate relationship with God as Father, which will completely satisfy our thirst.

A sense of emptiness is a common human experience. Rock star and humanitarian ambassador Bob Geldof was once asked whether he had found satisfaction: 'Not at all. I don't know what that would mean. I am unfulfilled as a human being. Otherwise, why are these large holes here [thumping his chest]? Everything I do is because I am frightened of being bored, because I know what is down there in those holes. I am frightened of it; it makes me depressed.'

How do you respond to what Bob Geldof says? Where do we tend to look to find satisfaction? Are you optimistic or cynical about the possibility of finding lasting fulfilment?

Cc STUDY

BLIND FAITH

According to biologist Richard Dawkins, 'Faith is the great cop-out, the great excuse to evade the need to think and evaluate evidence. Faith is belief in spite of, even perhaps because of, the lack of evidence.'

Do you agree that Christians believe without evidence? Is the Christian faith irrational?

READ: JOHN 9: 1-41 (PAGE 54)

WATCH: uncover.org.uk/john/video C

HISTORICAL CONTEXT

Opinions about Jesus are becoming sharply divided. Is he from God or is he a deluded troublemaker? The Pharisees, strict adherents of the Jewish religious law, are angry with him. In their view, Jesus doesn't keep the Sabbath, a day on which Jews are meant to refrain from any form of work in order to worship. But Jesus heals someone on the Sabbath, which, according to their traditions, was a break with the Sabbath regulations. They are so angry with Jesus that in the previous chapter they tried to murder him.

In this encounter, Jesus rejects the popular notion that a man's blindness is the result of his own or his parents' sin. Jesus heals the man on the Sabbath and is once again embroiled in controversy.

JOHN 9: 1-8

1   Describe what life would be like for someone born blind – practically, socially, emotionally. Note the hints in verses 1 and 8.

2   How might the man have felt as he walked to the pool? What might he have been thinking as he came back to the place where he was once forced to beg?

3 How does this miracle relate to Jesus' claiming to be the 'light of the world'? What does it suggest about the life that Jesus claims to offer?

Throughout his writing, John uses light primarily as a symbol of life, while darkness is symbolic of sin and death. This miracle depicts in actions what Jesus has come to do for the world. As the light of the world, Jesus claims to have come to rescue people from the darkness of sin and death and to give them eternal life.

JOHN 9:8-23

4 Why do you think the man's neighbours respond as they do? Why do they take him to the Pharisees in verses 8–13?

5 The Pharisees now enter the scene. Why can't they agree about what has happened, despite the clear testimony of the man? Read verses 13–17. What assumptions are guiding their conclusions?

6 Why are the man's parents now brought in? How do they respond, and why, in verses 18–23?

JOHN 9: 24-34

7 Why do you think the Pharisees react as they do to the man's testimony? Are they interested in 'the truth'?

8 How does the man respond to the accusations and insults of the Pharisees? What points does he make in verses 30–33?

JOHN 9:35-41

9 Why do you think Jesus seeks out the man?

10 In the last few hours, this man has experienced a radical re-evaluation of who he thinks Jesus is. How has his opinion changed in verses 11, 17 and 38, and what conclusion has he reached about Jesus' identity?

For the first time in this encounter, the man sees Jesus with his physical eyes and worships him. The man's journey from blindness to sight parallels his spiritual journey as he follows the evidence and comes to see who Jesus truly is. The term 'son of man' could just refer to another human being, but the Hebrew Scriptures use the term to describe a person with God-like characteristics.

11 This encounter begins with the assumption that the blind man is sinful. It ends in an incredibly unexpected way, with Jesus describing the Pharisees in this manner. What are they guilty of? What keeps them from accepting the conclusion to which the evidence points?

WHAT DOES THIS MEAN FOR US?

Jesus makes bold claims about himself in this passage. In claiming to be the 'light of the world', he insists that we are all in darkness without him. In the Hebrew Bible, worship is reserved for God alone, so by receiving the man's worship, Jesus has equated himself with God.

Oxford academic and author CS Lewis wrote about Jesus: 'You can shut him up as a fool, you can spit on him and kill him as a demon; or you can fall at his feet and call him Lord and God. But let us not come up with any patronizing nonsense about his being a great human teacher. He has not left that open to us. He didn't intend to.'

Why do you think people are more comfortable thinking about Jesus as a great teacher, but close their eyes to the kinds of claims he makes about himself in this encounter?

This session explores the painful topic of death.

<u>Why do you think it is a subject that we so often avoid talking openly about?</u>

READ:	JOHN 11:1-48 (PAGE 64)
WATCH:	uncover.org.uk/john/videoD

HISTORICAL CONTEXT

Jesus makes some bold claims about himself, not least that he is the Messiah, God's saviour of the world. In the previous chapter, he claims to be God's Son. The Jewish leaders are so outraged that they respond with murderous intent: 'We are not stoning you for any good work ... but for blasphemy, because you, a mere man, claim to be God' (John 10:33). They understand Jesus to mean that he claims to share the same nature as God, whom he calls his Father.

Jesus is now confronted with the death of a very close friend. Can he offer any hope in the face of death? Will he confirm his incredible claims to be God? What evidence is there to suggest that we should take his claim to be the saviour of the world seriously?

JOHN 11:1-16

1 What relationship does Jesus have with Lazarus and his family (see verses 2 and 5)? Why do you think they send for Jesus?

2 When Jesus hears about Lazarus' illness, what is so surprising about his response? What do the disciples fear will happen (verses 5–8)?

3 At what point does Jesus decide to go and see Lazarus? How do the disciples misunderstand what he says in verses 11–16?

4 It would seem utterly pointless for Jesus to walk for four days in order to see Lazarus now. What reason does Jesus give in verses 4 and 15 to explain his delay?

In the Hebrew Scriptures, 'glory' refers to the visible manifestation of God, usually in the form of radiance and splendour. Jesus says that, through what will happen at the home of Lazarus, the disciples are going to see that Jesus has the same glory, the same nature, as God. His deliberate delay in going to Bethany is for this purpose.

JOHN 11 : 17-27

5 Describe the scene that confronts Jesus when he arrives at the home of Lazarus. How do you think Mary and Martha feel? What do you think they expect Jesus to do? (See verses 17–24 and 30–33.)

6 What astonishing claim does Jesus make about himself in verses 25–26? According to Jesus, how is it possible for anyone to be confident of life after death?

JOHN 11 : 28 - 48

7 When Mary is made aware that Jesus has arrived, she goes out to meet him. What strikes you most about Jesus' response to her grief (verses 32–36)?

8 Jesus is said to be 'deeply moved in spirit and troubled' in verse 33 – literally 'angry' and 'outraged' in the original language. His grief is understandable, but why do you think he is so angry?

The Hebrew Scriptures teach that death was not part of the original human experience. As people turned away from God, the giver of life, their inevitable punishment was to experience death. Jesus is not only grieved by the death of a friend, he is also angry at the way in which death has caused so much pain in the world.

9 What was the crowd expecting to happen in verses 36–37? What was Martha expecting in verse 39?

10 What happens when Jesus calls Lazarus out of his tomb? How does this relate to his claim about himself in verses 25–26?

11 How does Jesus want people to respond to what they see (verses 41–42)? How do they actually respond (verses 45–48)?

WHAT DOES THIS MEAN FOR US?

After being diagnosed with terminal cancer, Apple founder Steve Jobs spoke of the inevitability of death: 'I can now say this to you with a bit more certainty than when death was a useful but purely intellectual concept. No one wants to die. Even people who want to go to heaven don't want to die to get there. And yet, death is the destination we all share. No one has ever escaped it.'

If what Jesus claims about himself is true, how might faith in him give us hope in the face of death, the 'destination we all share'?

Ee
STUDY

THE GREAT
EXCHANGE

Russian novelist and human rights campaigner
Alexander Solzhenitsyn considered the
hypothetical possibility of ridding the world
of evil people. He eventually came to the
conclusion that this would be impossible:
'The line dividing good and evil cuts through
the heart of every human being. And who is
willing to destroy a piece of his own heart?'

To what extent do you agree with this description of humanity?

READ: JOHN 19: 1-42 (PAGE 106)

WATCH: uncover.org.uk/john/video E

HISTORICAL CONTEXT

The religious leaders are resolved to put Jesus to death for blasphemy, because Jesus has claimed to be the divine saviour of the world. An opportunity arrives when Judas, one of Jesus' disciples, agrees to betray him. In the hours before this account, Jesus has been arrested and evidence fabricated in order to condemn him. Only the occupying Roman authorities can inflict the death penalty, so the Roman governor Pontius Pilate has to be persuaded of Jesus' guilt.

The religious leaders know that Pilate will have no interest in being dragged into their religious quarrel. In order to secure Jesus' condemnation, they try to persuade Pilate that the preacher from Galilee should be executed on the grounds of treason.

JOHN 19: 1-16

1   Describe the attitude of the soldiers towards Jesus. Why are they mocking him?

2   What does Pilate emphasise about Jesus as a result of his interrogation of him in verses 4, 6 and 12?

3   Why does Pilate become afraid when he hears the charges brought against Jesus in verses 7–8?

4 Jesus is before the man who has the power to execute him. What strikes you about Pilate and Jesus in their interchange in verses 9–11?

5 Read verses 12–16. Pilate hopes to set Jesus free. How are the religious leaders finally able to persuade Pilate to sentence Jesus to death?

JOHN 19: 17-27

6 Jesus has been interrogated, mocked and badly beaten. He is now forced to carry his cross through the crowded streets of Jerusalem. What do you imagine his physical condition to be?

In one short sentence, John tells us that Jesus was crucified. Yet crucifixion was one of the most horrific punishments imaginable. It was used as the ultimate deterrent to rebellion against Rome. Notices that gave the reasons for crucifixion were therefore nailed above those being executed. Jewish law added to the humiliation of crucifixion by stating that anyone killed in this way was considered cursed by God.

7 Standing near to the cross are Jesus' mother and a handful of followers (verses 25–27). What do you think they are feeling? What are they thinking about Jesus' claim to be the divine saviour and his offer of life?

JOHN 19: 28-42

8 Everything suggests that Jesus is utterly ruined. Yet what hints are there that Jesus believes he is still truly in control (verses 28 and 30)?

As John reports the events of Jesus' crucifixion, he continually refers to the fulfilment of Old Testament predictions of what would happen to the Messiah. Isaiah (writing in c.700 BC) describes what would happen and what it would mean for the world:

He was despised and rejected by mankind,
a man of suffering, and familiar with pain.
Like one from whom people hide their faces
he was despised, and we held him in low esteem.

Surely he took up our pain
and bore our suffering,
yet we considered him punished by God,
stricken by him, and afflicted.
But he was pierced for our transgressions,
he was crushed for our iniquities;
the punishment that brought us peace was on him,
and by his wounds we are healed.
We all, like sheep, have gone astray,
each of us has turned to our own way;
and the LORD has laid on him
the iniquity of us all (Isaiah 53:3–6).

9 How do these words reflect what Jesus is experiencing? According to Isaiah, what problem would the Messiah come to address, and how would he achieve it?

Before he dies, Jesus says 'I am thirsty'. In John's Gospel, thirst is a metaphor for our alienation from God because of our sin. At this point Jesus is experiencing God's judgement, but not for his own sins – he is innocent, as Pilate has said repeatedly. The punishment of alienation and death that we deserve is being laid on him so that we can enjoy peace with God.

10 With his final breath, Jesus cries out, 'It is finished.' What do you think Jesus believes his death on the cross is achieving?

11 Nicodemus, a distinguished religious teacher, embalms Jesus' body with a huge quantity of spices. Such an amount would normally be reserved for kings. Why is it so surprising that Nicodemus wishes to give Jesus such a burial?

WHAT DOES THIS MEAN FOR US?

Author Tim Keller understands the crucifixion to be the unique element of Christianity in which Jesus substitutes himself for us. He is innocent but bears in his own death God's judgement on our sins. In this way he is the saviour of the world.

Keller writes, 'The founders of every other major religion essentially came as teachers, not as saviours. They came to say: "Do this and you will find the divine." But Jesus came essentially as a saviour rather than a teacher (though he was that as well). Jesus says "I am the divine come to you, to do what you could not do for yourselves." The Christian message is that we are saved not by our record, but by Christ's record.'

Given what you have learned about the death of Jesus, is Tim Keller right? Is the essence of the cross one of salvation, in which God pays the price we should have paid?

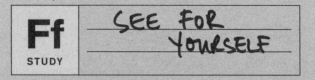

Ff
STUDY

SEE FOR YOURSELF

Confirmation bias is the tendency to interpret new evidence as confirmation of one's existing beliefs or theories. Why do you think people can sometimes be resistant to questioning and changing their existing beliefs?

What kind of evidence would you need in order to change your mind about something?

READ:	JOHN 20:1-29 (PAGE 114)
WATCH:	uncover.org.uk/john/video F

HISTORICAL CONTEXT

Jesus has suffered a hideous death: crucifixion for blasphemy because he claimed to be the Son of God. What's more, he insisted on giving his life in this way in order to experience God's judgement on the sins of others. But now he lies dead in a borrowed tomb. Were his offers of life merely words? Is this the end of the Jesus movement? His disciples think so. Grief-stricken and afraid, they hide themselves away, uncertain of their own future now that Jesus is dead.

Joseph of Arimathea and Nicodemus laid the body in Joseph's family tomb. The custom was to cover a body with spices, wrap it in linen and seal it in the tomb until the flesh had rotted away. About a year later the remains would have been recovered and transferred to a second burial place (an ossuary). There the story of Jesus would have ended, a dead Messiah was no Messiah at all.

But here we are, still talking about him...

JOHN 20:1-18

1 Imagine how the disciples must have been feeling in the days after Jesus' death. How might they reflect on the last three years with Jesus? What might their thoughts be about their future?

2 Mary goes to the tomb and finds that the large stone that had been placed across the entrance to prevent anyone from stealing the body has been rolled away. What conclusion does she reach about what has happened to the body?

3 Peter and the other disciple arrive at the tomb. They find that the body is gone, just as Mary has described. What are the possible explanations for this?

4 What do you think the other disciple sees in the tomb that convinces him that something more is going on than simply a grave robbery?

5 Mary remains standing outside the tomb. What is the cause of her distress? Read verses 11–15: what possibilities is she open to? What convinces her that Jesus is alive with her?

6 The pagan philosopher Celsus ridiculed Christians for having a 'hysterical woman' as their key witness to the resurrection. He was not alone; at this time, women were not acceptable as legal witnesses. What does it suggest about Jesus that he chose to present himself alive to Mary first? Does this suggest anything about the reliability of John's account itself?

JOHN 20: 19-20, 24-29

7 The disciples are now in hiding, fearing for their lives. Suddenly they are aware of Jesus standing among them. What conclusions do they reach about what they see? What do you think is the significance of Jesus' showing them his hands and side?

8 What is Thomas' reaction? Do you think it is a reasonable response? Why or why not?

9 Thomas is clearly sceptical concerning the disciples' claims to have seen Jesus. What persuades him to change his beliefs?

10 Why do you think Thomas goes beyond accepting that Jesus is alive to believing that he is God ('My Lord and my God!')? You might want to refer back to our very first study, specifically the quotation from Isaiah 25 concerning what God would do when he came to the world.

11 What is Jesus' response to Thomas' worship? What does this tell us about Jesus?

Jesus' words to Thomas in verse 29 may be a mild rebuke; Thomas should have believed what the disciples told him. Jesus points to the fact that, in the future, people will believe without seeing.

12 Is there a difference between believing without seeing and believing without evidence? What does John hope that the effect of his account will be on us, his readers?

WHAT DOES THIS MEAN FOR US?

John shows us people who are sceptical and do not expect the resurrection. Mary, the disciples, Peter, Thomas … they are all presented with evidence and are compelled to change their whole way of thinking.

As we come to the end of John's account of Jesus' life, is there anything that is keeping you from accepting the resurrection and believing that Jesus is the Christ and the Son of God, and receiving the life that he promises?

Baptise: To immerse someone in water as a sign of being made clean from sin and being given new life from God. (See Sin)

Disciples: The word used for the followers of John the Baptist and Jesus. Disciple literally means 'learner' or 'pupil'.

Festivals: Each year the Jews celebrated significant events in their history. The Festival of Shelters celebrated God's guidance when their forefathers lived in shelters after escaping from Egypt; the Festival of Dedication (Hannukah) celebrated the return to the temple for worship after it had been destroyed and rebuilt.

Gentile: A term used to describe anyone who was not a Jew.

Glory: Glory refers to the visible manifestation of God's splendour and the honour given to God by those who worship him. Jesus reveals God's glory in his life (seen through his miracles) and in his death (seen in his love for a world that rejected him).

Holy Spirit: The Holy Spirit is God, just as much as God the Father and Jesus are. He continues Jesus' work and teaching after his death and resurrection.

John the Baptist (see Baptise): A relative of Jesus who, like a royal official, prepared the way for Jesus' arrival.

Lamb of God: In Jewish religion, lambs were sacrificed as a substitute, the innocent lamb symbolically bearing the guilt of sin in the place of a sinful person. Jesus is described as the fulfilment of this symbolic sacrifice, the true 'Lamb of God' who is punished in the place of the guilty, making forgiveness and a relationship with God possible.

Manna: Manna means 'what is it' in Hebrew. Centuries before Jesus, the Jewish people had left Egypt and, as they journeyed through the desert, God miraculously provided them with a bread-like food, called manna.

Messiah/Christ: 'The anointed one' – meaning someone who is specially chosen and sent by God, to rescue his people and to reign over them. At the time of Jesus, many were waiting for God's special rescuer-king to arrive.

Moses and the Law: Moses was a Jewish leader who led the people of Israel out of slavery in Egypt and who was given the Ten Commandments. His writing is the basis of the first five books of the Old Testament, known as the Law. (The Old Testament is the part of the Bible written before Jesus' time on earth.)

Passover: An annual religious festival which celebrated God's rescue of the people of Israel from slavery in Egypt.

Pharisees: A religious group who were well known for their purity and careful attention to Jewish laws and customs. They added many of their own laws to God's law.

Prophet: Someone who spoke God's truth to the people. One of the great prophets, Moses, had promised that an even greater prophet would come one day.

Sabbath: The seventh and holy day of the Jewish week, beginning at sunset on the Friday. It was a day of rest when no work could be done.

Samaritans: A mixed-race people, living in central Israel, who were despised by the Jews as an inferior racial and religious group.

Saviour: A rescuer. Jesus rescues those who believe in him, both Jews and non-Jews, from the coming judgment.

Scriptures: The name for the writings of the Jewish faith. They contained many predictions about the coming Messiah.

Sin: The word used by the Bible to describe humanity's rebellion against God and our determination to live without him. In John's Gospel the clearest sign of this rebellion is refusing to believe in Jesus.

Son of Man: The Old Testament refers to a person coming in the future who will be given universal authority by God. Jesus claims to be the one with this power and authority.

Temple: Located in Jerusalem, the temple represented the symbolic presence of God living in the centre of his people. It was the place of Jewish worship. Jesus claimed to have replaced the temple because in meeting him, people encountered the living God. The temple was finally destroyed by the Romans in AD70.

uccf:thechristianunions

This resource is produced by UCCF: The Christian Unions. UCCF is made up of hundreds of university Christian Unions across Britain. We exist to give every student on campus an opportunity to hear about Jesus. This resource has been developed to help you engage with the narrative of John's Gospel. To find out more about Christian Unions, visit www.uccf.org.uk.

Contact

UCCF: The Christian Unions
Blue Boar House
5 Blue Boar St
Oxford
OX1 4EE

T: 01865 253678
E: email@uccf.org.uk
W: uccf.org.uk

Registered Charity No. 306137

 facebook.com/uccf.thechristianunions

twitter.com/uccf

 youtube.com/uccfmedia